This book belongs to:

Welcome Woman of God!

How to use this Journal

Dear Woman of God,

Welcome again to your new prayer journal. I created this journal with daily sections for prayer and the word to help you strengthen your walk with God and build a prayer habit day by day. Here is a how to guide to help you get the most out of your prayer journal.

This **Prayer Journal** is equipped with **daily prayer pages**. They feature:

- Space to note bible verses that speak you,
- Lines to start your day with praise,
- Boxes for confessions and thanksgiving,
- Space for your prayer requests

And lastly a section for you write to down each day the prayers God has answered.

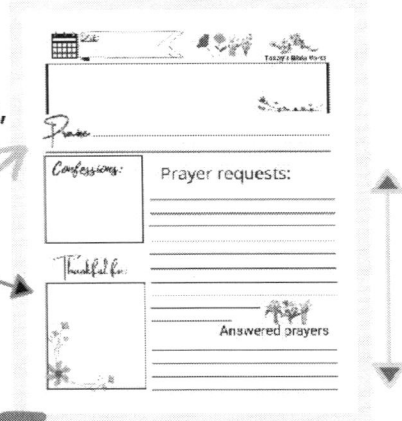

All done in style so that your journal always looks good with minimal effort and so you can focus on your relationship with God
~ he main thing!

This Journal also includes a copy of **The Lord's prayer** in the back and **Weekly Topics** with relevant scriptures for you to focus on during the week. I recommend that you find and write down bible verses on the weekly topic and then focus on it during your prayers to in addition to your usual, pressing / personal prayers to add some rotation & variety. These are long-term topics...

for prayer so I hope you will find these weekly topics useful if not helpful!

Some examples of topics are;
- Salvation
- Love
- Favour
- Wisdom
- Rest & Peace
- Grace
- and Protection

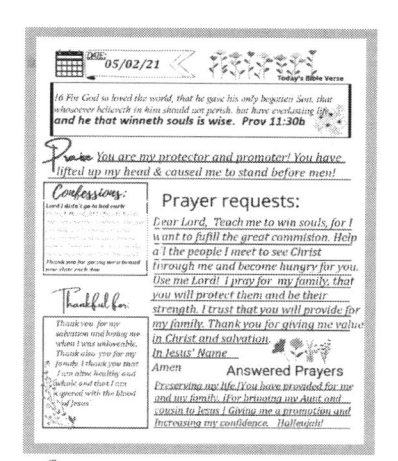

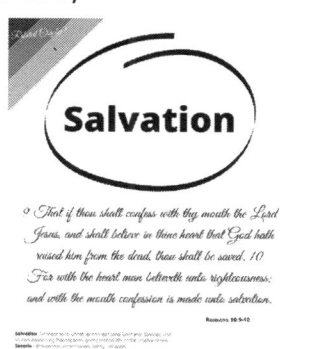

Here's an example I've filled out for salvation!

The daily prayer pages alternate slightly in their floral design to add a little variety. The journal also features,

believe

three pages for testimonies that I pray you will be able to fill to bursting, In Jesus' Name, Amen!

Good Luck & God bless!

Gloria ~

Amazon.com   Amazon.co.uk

For more books by Gloria, please scan the QR Codes:-

love

Related Chapter!

Salvation

9 That if thou shalt confess with thy mouth the Lord Jesus, and shalt believe in thine heart that God hath raised him from the dead, thou shalt be saved. 10 For with the heart man believeth unto righteousness; and with the mouth confession is made unto salvation.

Romans 10:9-10

Salvation -To know Jesus Christ as your personal Lord and Saviour, and so now possessing [having been given] eternal life; In the original Greek - **Soteria** - deliverance, preservation, safety, salvation

DATE:

Today's Bible Verse

Praise

Confessions:

Prayer requests:

Thankful for:

Answered prayers

DATE:

Today's Bible Verse

Praise _____
_____

Confessions:

Prayer requests:
_____
_____
_____
_____
_____
_____
_____
_____
_____
_____

Thankful for:

Answered prayers
_____
_____
_____
_____

DATE:

Today's Bible Verse

Praise

Confessions:

Prayer requests:

Thankful for:

Answered prayers

DATE:

Today's Bible Verse

Praise _____

Confessions:

Prayer requests:

_____
_____
_____
_____
_____
_____
_____

Thankful for:

_____
_____

Answered prayers

_____
_____
_____

DATE:

Today's Bible Verse

Praise

Confessions:

Prayer requests:

Thankful for:

Answered prayers

DATE:

Today's Bible Verse

Praise _____

Confessions:

Thankful for:

Prayer requests:
_____
_____
_____
_____
_____
_____
_____
_____
_____

Answered prayers
_____
_____
_____
_____

DATE:

Today's Bible Verse

Praise _____

Confessions:

Thankful for:

Prayer requests:

_____
_____
_____
_____
_____
_____
_____
_____
_____
_____
_____
_____

Answered prayers

_____
_____
_____
_____

Joy

6 Rejoice evermore.

1 Thessalonians 5:16

13 Now the God of hope fill you with all joy and peace in believing, that ye may abound in hope, through the power of the Holy Ghost.

Romans 15:13

...for this day is holy unto our Lord: neither be ye sorry; for the joy of the Lord is your strength.

Nehemiah 8:10b

DATE:

Today's Bible Verse

Praise _____

Confessions:

Prayer requests:

_____
_____
_____
_____
_____
_____
_____

Thankful for:

_____

Answered Prayers

_____
_____
_____
_____

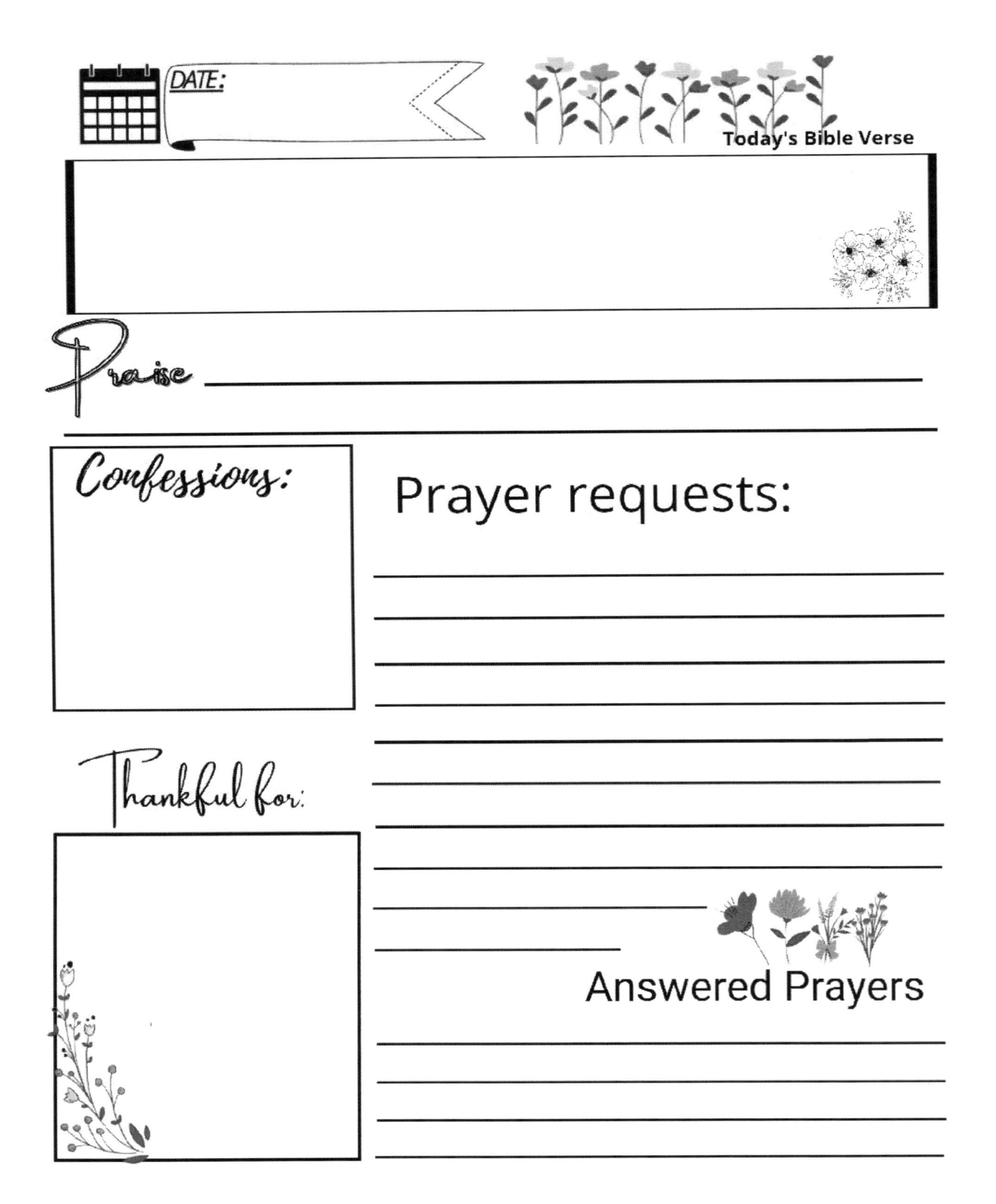

DATE:

Today's Bible Verse

Praise _____

Confessions:

Prayer requests:

Thankful for:

Answered Prayers

DATE:

Today's Bible Verse

Praise _____

Confessions:

Prayer requests:

_____
_____
_____
_____
_____
_____

Thankful for:

_____
_____
_____

Answered Prayers

_____
_____
_____
_____

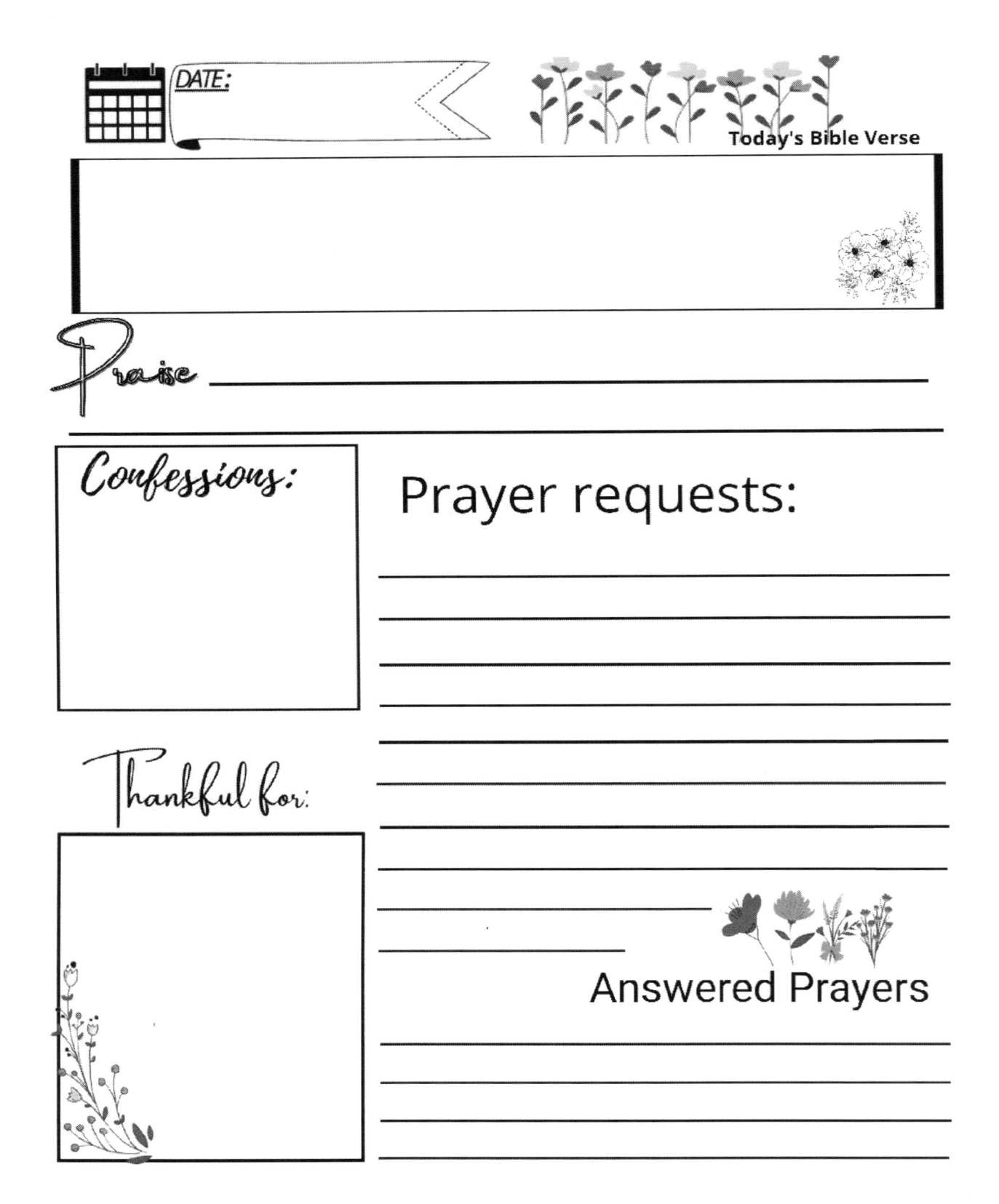

DATE:

Today's Bible Verse

Praise _____

Confessions:

Prayer requests:

Thankful for:

Answered Prayers

DATE:

Today's Bible Verse

Praise _____

Confessions:

Prayer requests:

_____
_____
_____
_____
_____
_____
_____

Thankful for:

_____

Answered Prayers

_____
_____
_____
_____

DATE:

Today's Bible Verse

Praise _____

Confessions:

Prayer requests:
_____
_____
_____
_____
_____
_____
_____

Thankful for:

_____
_____

Answered Prayers
_____
_____
_____

DATE:

Today's Bible Verse

Praise _____

Confessions:

Prayer requests:

_____
_____
_____
_____
_____
_____
_____

Thankful for:

_____

Answered Prayers

_____
_____
_____
_____

Protection

Psalm 91

7 A thousand shall fall at thy side, and ten thousand at thy right hand; but it shall not come nigh theee

8 Only with thine eyes shalt thou behold and see the reward of the wicked.

9 Because thou hast made the Lord, which is my refuge, even the most High, thy habitation;

10 There shall no evil befall thee, neither shall any plague come nigh thy dwelling.

11 For he shall give his angels charge over thee, to keep thee in all thy ways.

Psalm 91:7-11

DATE:

Today's Bible Verse

Praise

Confessions:

Prayer requests:

Thankful for:

Answered prayers

DATE:

Today's Bible Verse

Praise _____

Confessions:

Prayer requests:

Thankful for:

Answered prayers

DATE:

Today's Bible Verse

Praise _____

Confessions:

Prayer requests:
_____
_____
_____
_____
_____
_____
_____
_____

Thankful for:

_____
_____

Answered prayers
_____
_____
_____
_____

DATE:

Today's Bible Verse

Praise

Confessions:

Prayer requests:

Thankful for:

Answered prayers

DATE:

Today's Bible Verse

Praise

Confessions:

Prayer requests:

Thankful for:

Answered prayers

DATE:

Today's Bible Verse

Praise _____

Confessions:

Prayer requests:
_____
_____
_____
_____
_____
_____
_____

Thankful for:

_____
_____

Answered prayers
_____
_____
_____
_____

DATE:

Today's Bible Verse

Praise _____

Confessions:

Prayer requests:
_____
_____
_____
_____
_____
_____
_____

Thankful for:

_____

Answered prayers
_____
_____
_____
_____

Grace

8 For by grace are ye saved through faith; and that not of yourselves: it is the gift of God: 9 Not of works, lest any man should boast.

-Ephesians 2:8-9

DATE:

Today's Bible Verse

Praise _____

Confessions:

Prayer requests:

Thankful for:

Answered Prayers

DATE:

Today's Bible Verse

Praise _____

Confessions:

Prayer requests:
_____
_____
_____
_____
_____
_____
_____
_____

Thankful for:

_____

Answered Prayers
_____
_____
_____
_____

DATE:

Today's Bible Verse

Praise _____

Confessions:

Prayer requests:
_____
_____
_____
_____
_____
_____
_____
_____
_____

Thankful for:

Answered Prayers
_____
_____
_____
_____

DATE:

Today's Bible Verse

Praise _____

Confessions:

Prayer requests:

Thankful for:

Answered Prayers

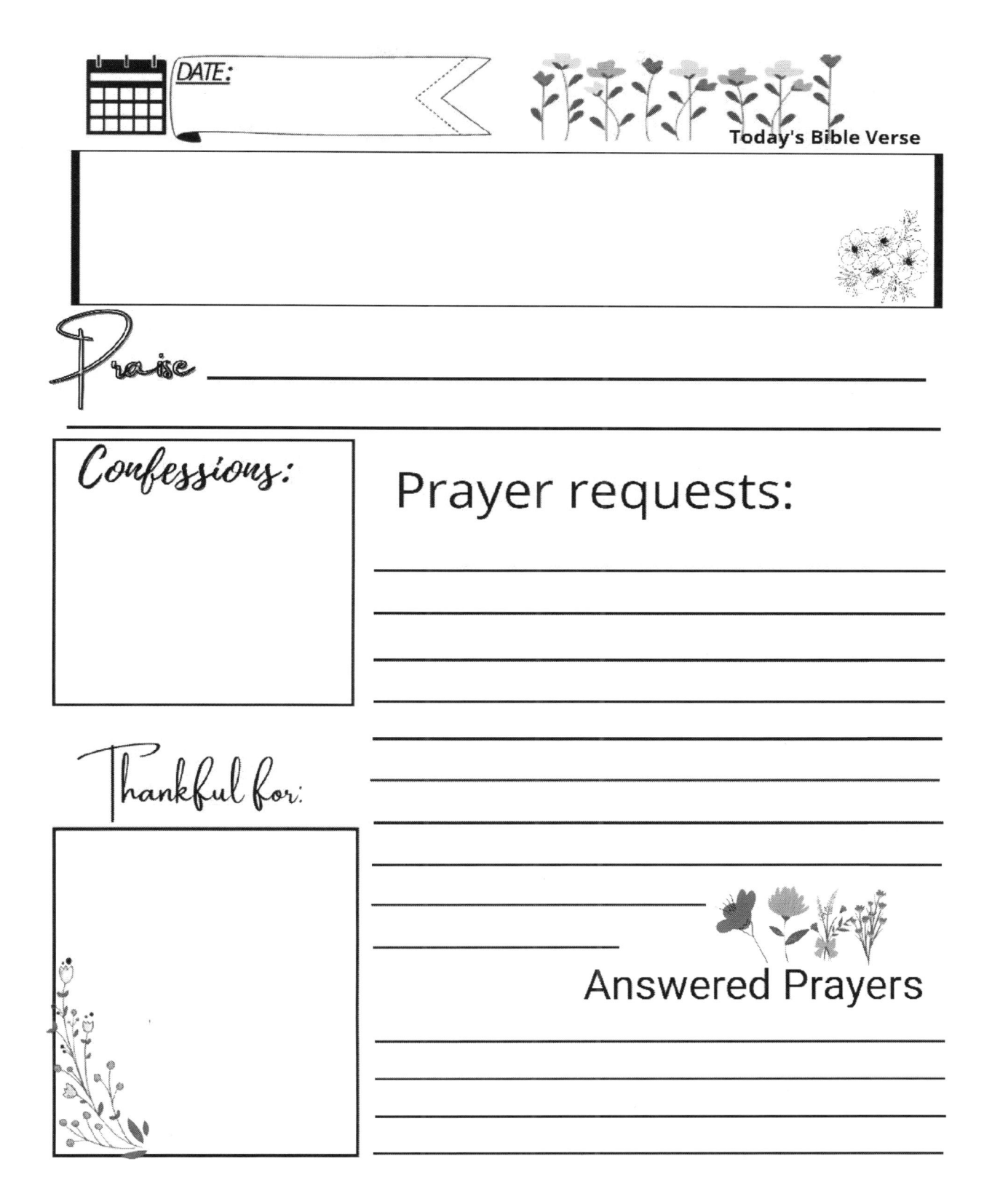

DATE:

Today's Bible Verse

Praise _____

Confessions:

Prayer requests:

_____
_____
_____
_____
_____
_____
_____
_____
_____

Thankful for:

Answered Prayers

_____
_____
_____
_____

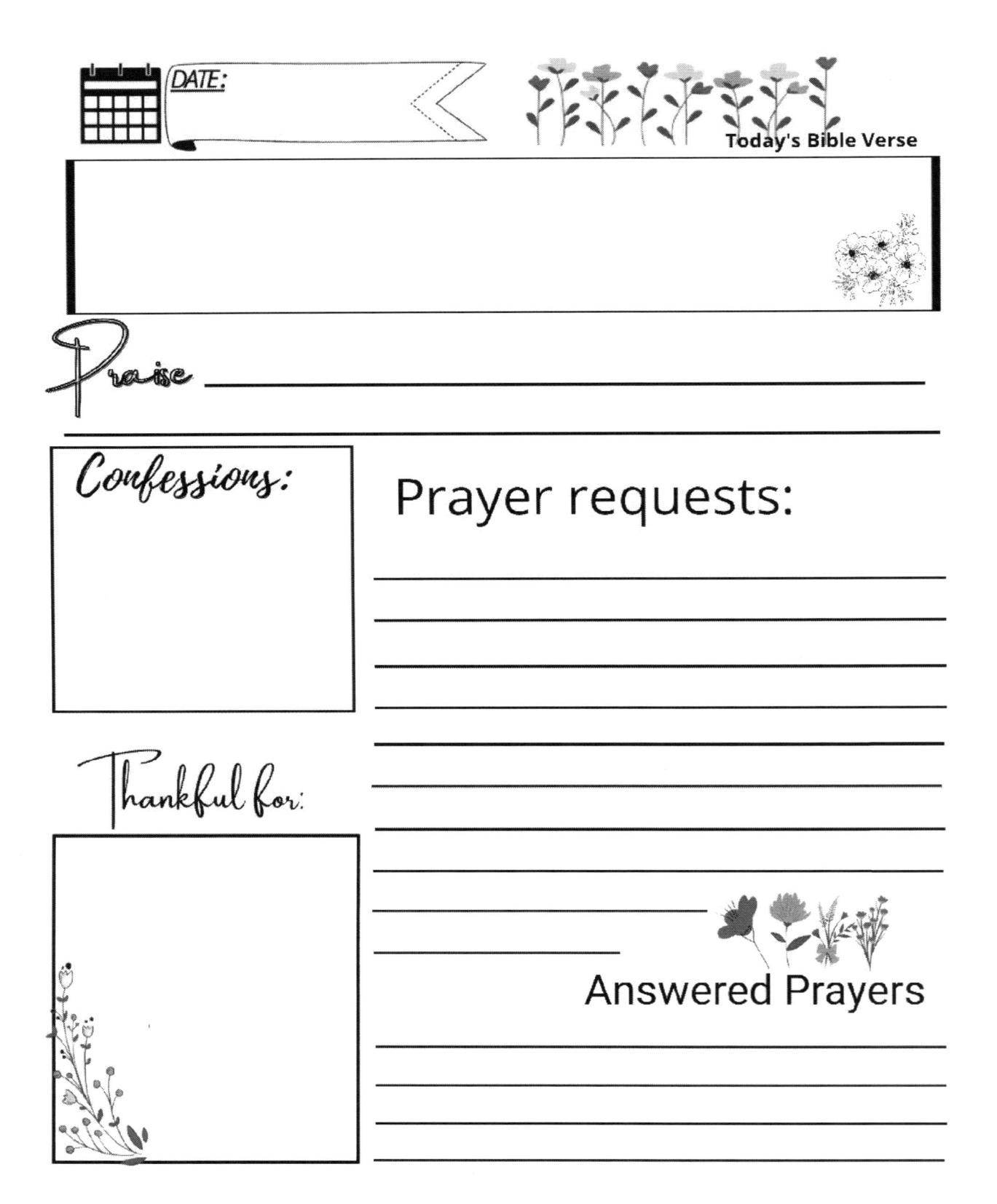

DATE:

Today's Bible Verse

Praise _____

Confessions:

Prayer requests:
_____
_____
_____
_____
_____
_____
_____

Thankful for:

_____
_____

Answered Prayers
_____
_____
_____

DATE:

Today's Bible Verse

Praise _____

Confessions:

Prayer requests:

Thankful for:

Answered Prayers

Wisdom

7 Wisdom is the principal thing; therefore get wisdom: and with all thy getting get understanding.

Proverbs 4:7

DATE:

Today's Bible Verse

Praise _____

Confessions:

Thankful for:

Prayer requests:

_____
_____
_____
_____
_____
_____
_____
_____
_____

Answered prayers

_____
_____
_____
_____

DATE:

Today's Bible Verse

Praise _____

Confessions:

Prayer requests:
_____
_____
_____
_____
_____
_____
_____
_____
_____
_____
_____

Thankful for:

Answered prayers
_____
_____
_____
_____

DATE:

Today's Bible Verse

Praise _____

Confessions:

Prayer requests:
_____
_____
_____
_____
_____
_____
_____
_____

Thankful for:

_____
_____

Answered prayers

_____
_____
_____
_____

DATE:

Today's Bible Verse

Praise _____

Confessions:

Prayer requests:

Thankful for:

Answered prayers

DATE:

Today's Bible Verse

Praise _____

Confessions:

Prayer requests:

Thankful for:

Answered prayers

DATE:

Today's Bible Verse

Praise _____

Confessions:

Prayer requests:

Thankful for:

Answered prayers

DATE:

Today's Bible Verse

Praise _____

Confessions:

Prayer requests:
_____
_____
_____
_____
_____
_____

Thankful for:

_____
_____

Answered prayers
_____
_____
_____
_____

Favour!

5 For his anger endureth but a moment; in his favour is life: weeping may endure for a night, but joy cometh in the morning.

Psalm 30:5

15 Now when the turn of Esther, the daughter of Abihail the uncle of Mordecai, who had taken her for his daughter, was come to go in unto the king, she required nothing but what Hegai the king's chamberlain, the keeper of the women, appointed. And Esther* obtained favour in the sight of all them that looked upon her.

Esther 2:15

*I like to put my name there when I'm reading out loud, to make it a prophetic prayer. Try it!

DATE:

Today's Bible Verse

Praise _____

Confessions:

Prayer requests:

Thankful for:

Answered Prayers

DATE:

Today's Bible Verse

Praise _____

Confessions:

Prayer requests:
_____
_____
_____
_____
_____
_____
_____

Thankful for:

_____
_____

Answered Prayers
_____
_____
_____
_____

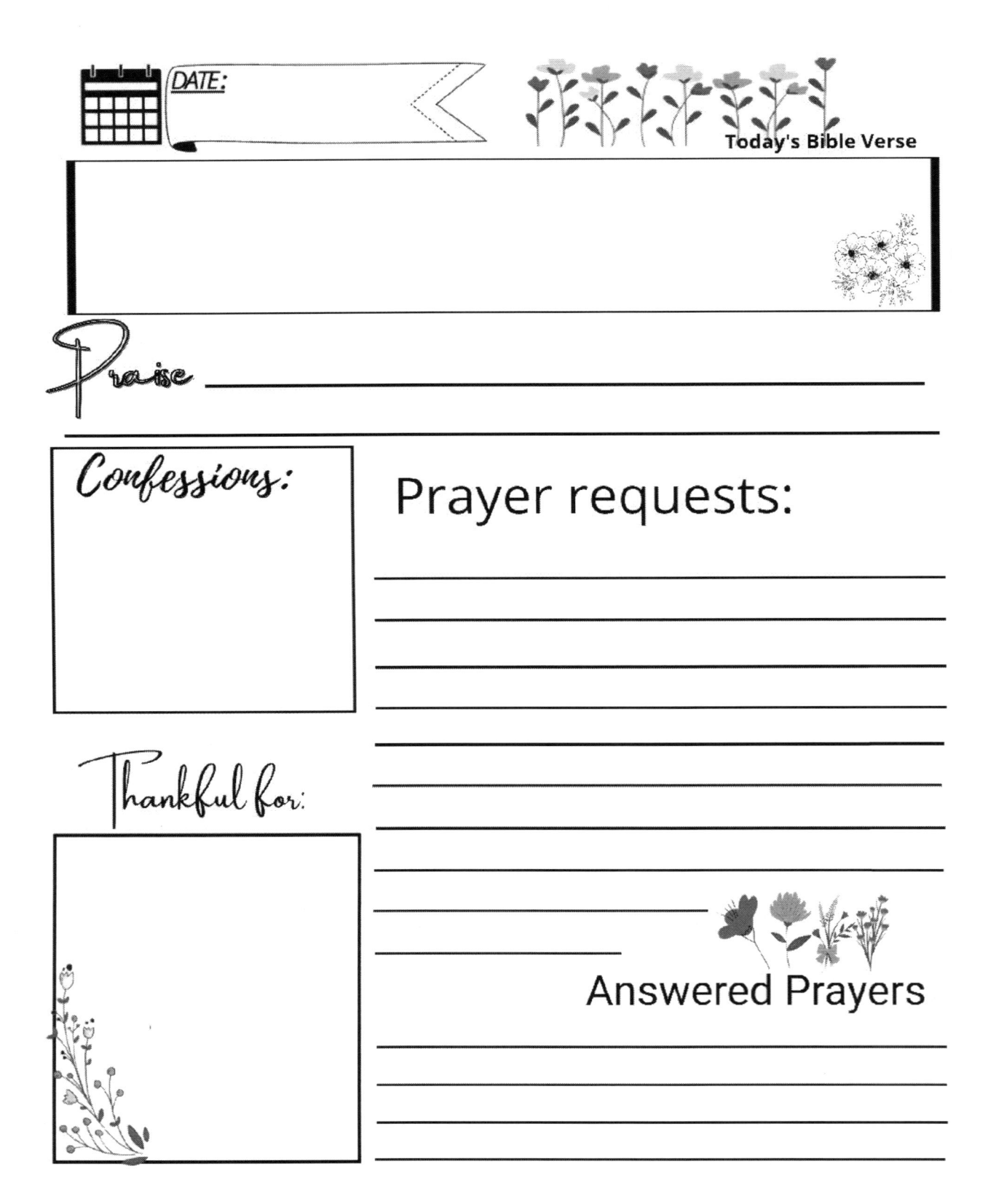

DATE:

Today's Bible Verse

Praise _____

Confessions:

Prayer requests:
_____
_____
_____
_____
_____
_____
_____

Thankful for:

_____

Answered Prayers
_____
_____
_____
_____

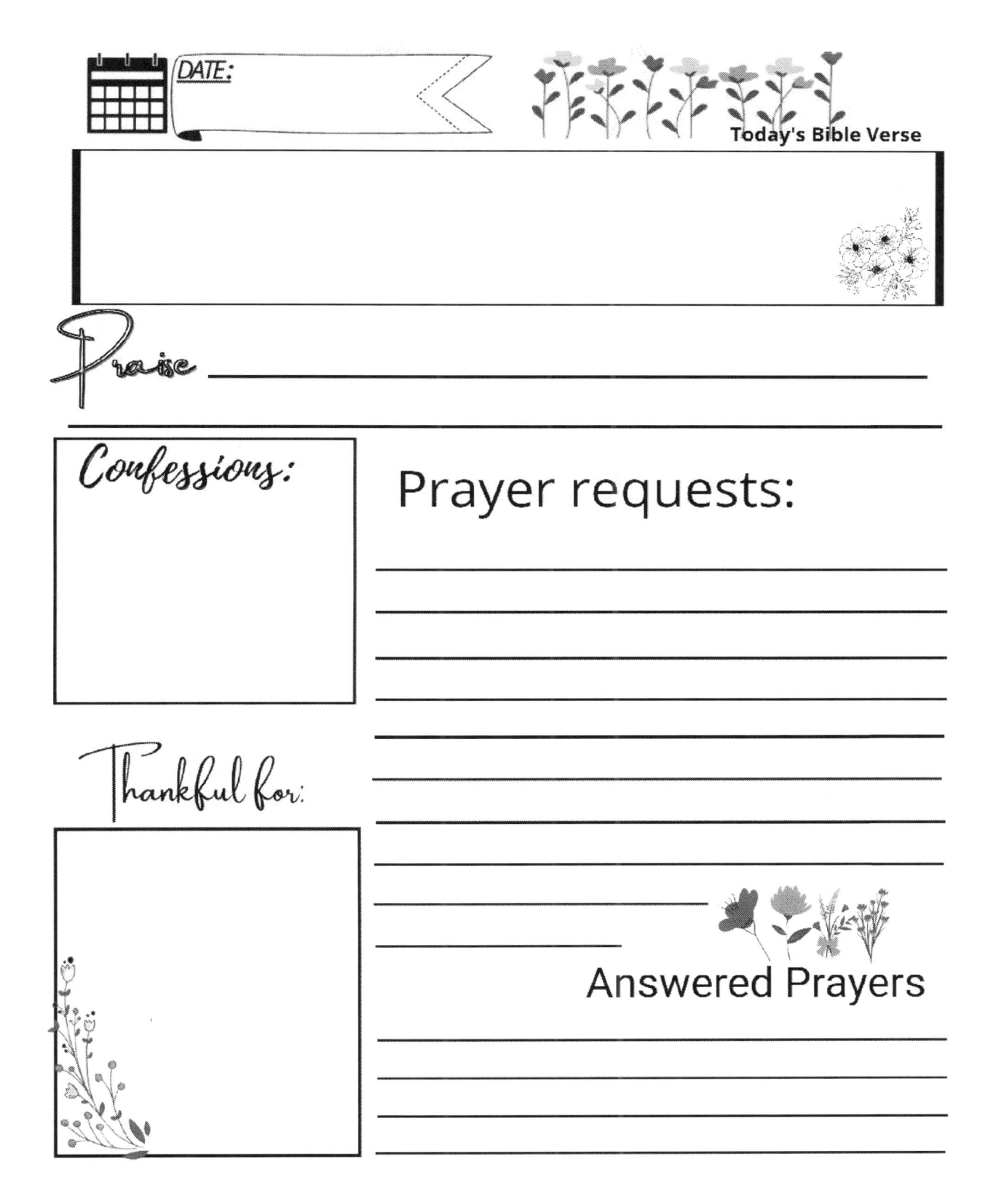

DATE:

Today's Bible Verse

Praise _____

Confessions:

Prayer requests:

Thankful for:

Answered Prayers

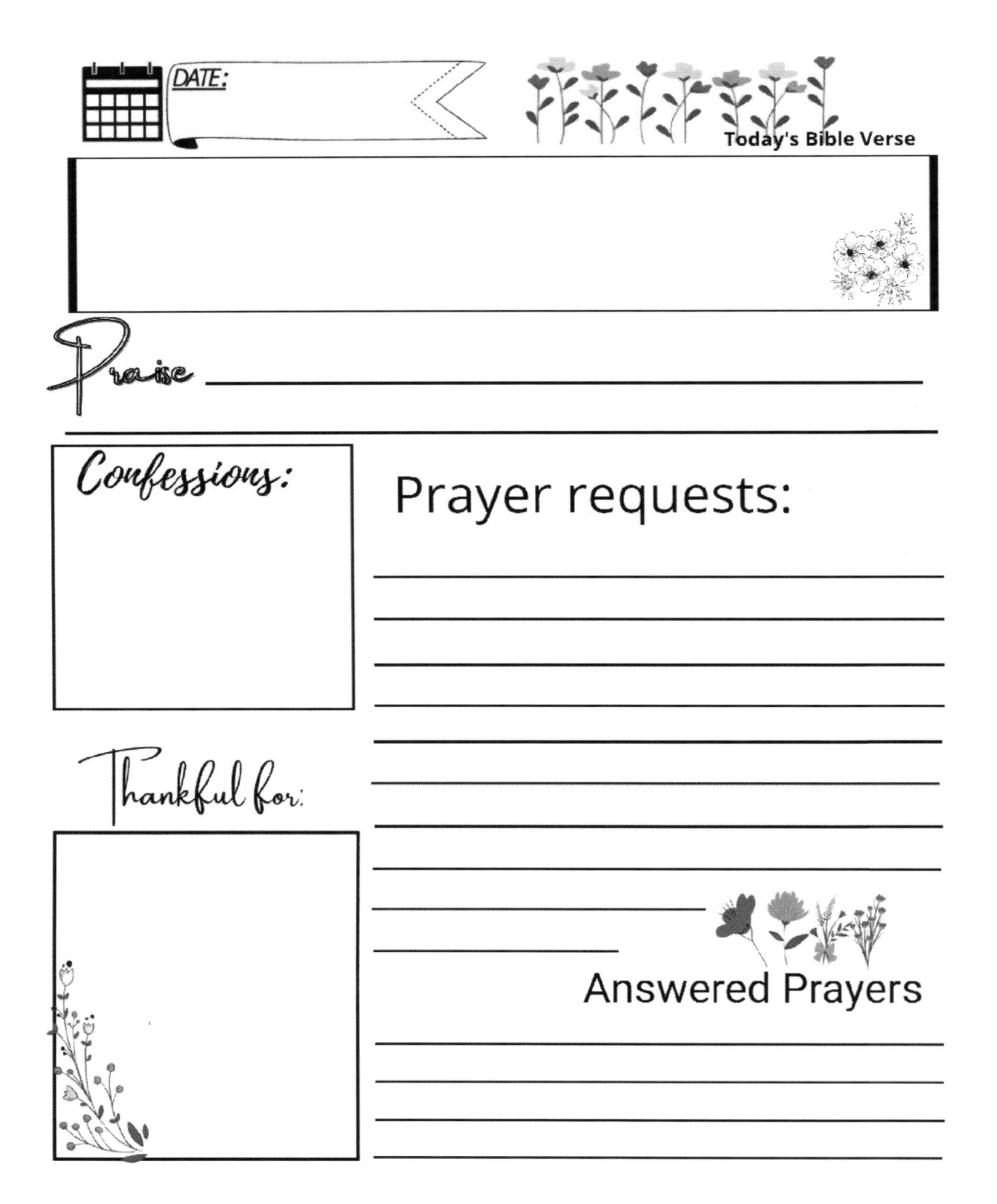

DATE:

Today's Bible Verse

Praise _____

Confessions:

Thankful for:

Prayer requests:

_____
_____
_____
_____
_____
_____
_____
_____

Answered Prayers

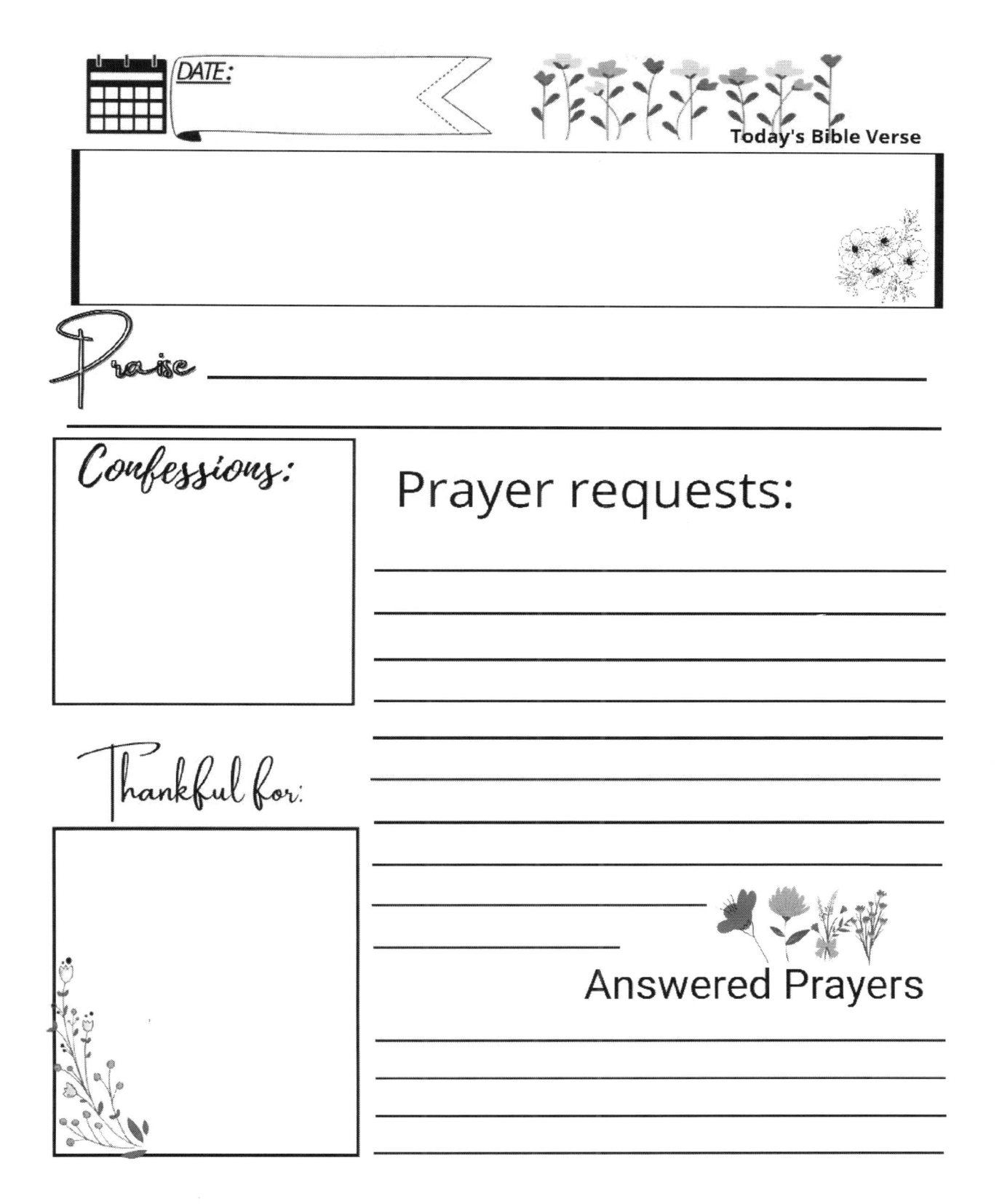

_____
_____
_____
_____

DATE:

Today's Bible Verse

Praise _____

Confessions:

Prayer requests:

Thankful for:

Answered Prayers

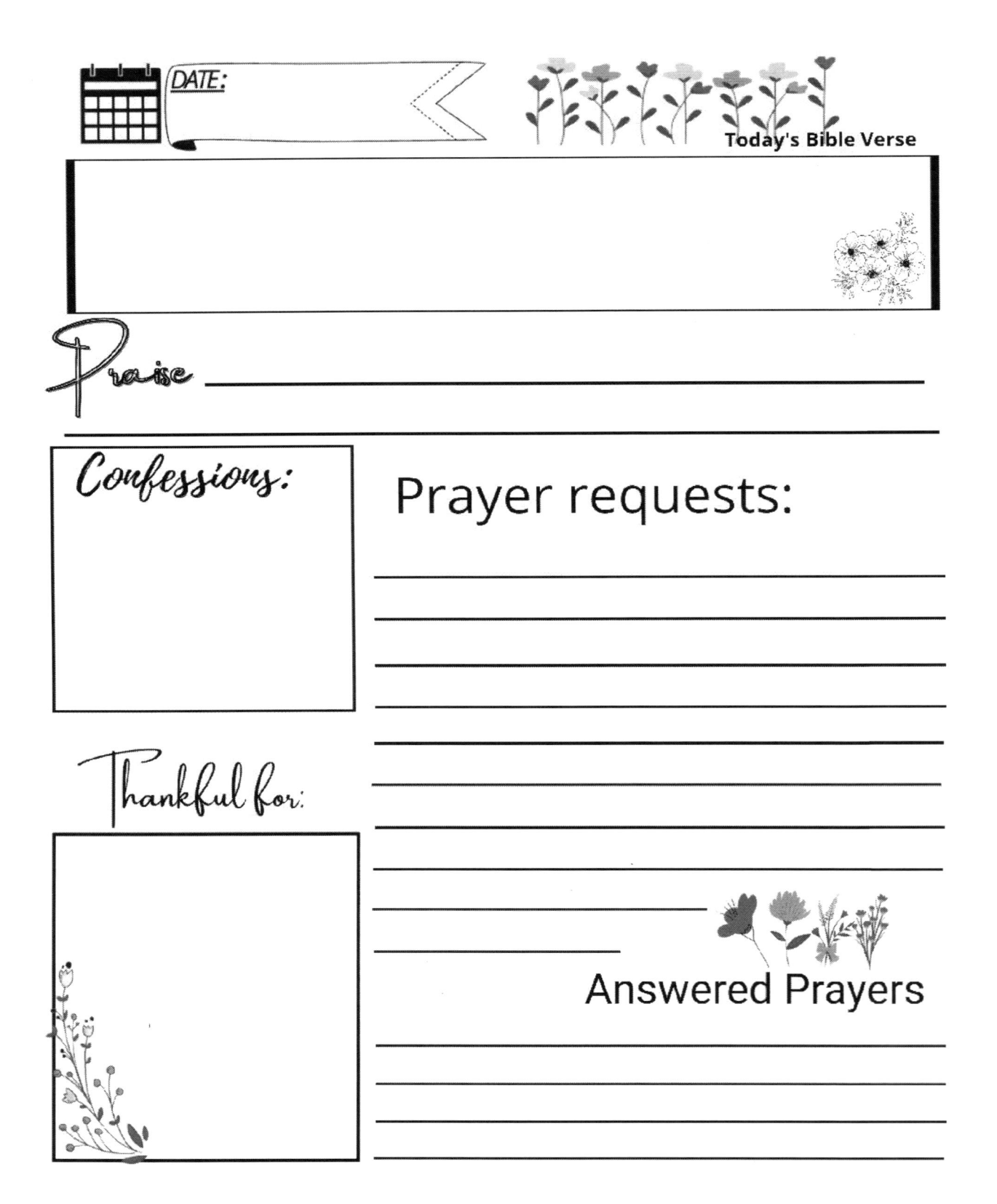

DATE:

Today's Bible Verse

Praise _____

Confessions:

Prayer requests:

_____
_____
_____
_____
_____
_____
_____
_____

Thankful for:

_____
_____

Answered Prayers

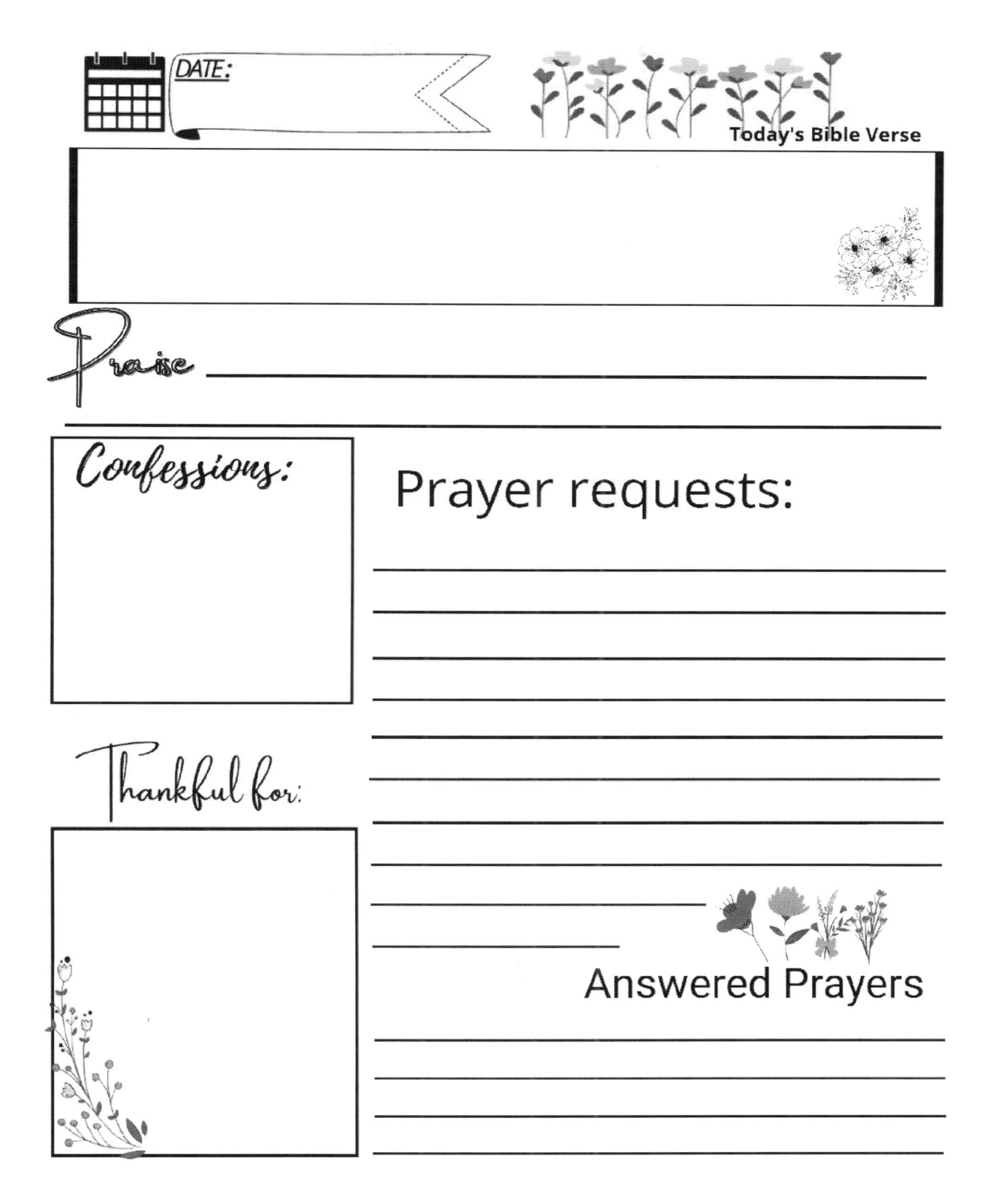

_____
_____
_____
_____

Related Chapter!

Love

13 And now abideth faith, hope, charity, these three; but the greatest of these is charity*.

1 Corinthians 13:13

| *unconditional divine love, agapē |

DATE:

Today's Bible Verse

Praise

Confessions:

Prayer requests:

Thankful for:

Answered prayers

DATE:

Today's Bible Verse

Praise _____

Confessions:

Thankful for:

Prayer requests:

_____
_____
_____
_____
_____
_____
_____
_____

Answered prayers

_____
_____
_____
_____

DATE:

Today's Bible Verse

Praise _____

Confessions:

Prayer requests:

Thankful for:

Answered prayers

DATE:

Today's Bible Verse

Praise _____

Confessions:

Prayer requests:
_____
_____
_____
_____
_____
_____
_____
_____
_____

Thankful for:

Answered prayers
_____
_____
_____
_____

DATE:

Today's Bible Verse

Praise

Confessions:

Prayer requests:

Thankful for:

Answered prayers

DATE:

Today's Bible Verse

Praise _____

Confessions:

Prayer requests:

_____
_____
_____
_____
_____
_____
_____
_____

Thankful for:

_____
_____

Answered prayers

_____
_____
_____
_____

DATE:

Today's Bible Verse

Praise

Confessions:

Prayer requests:

Thankful for:

Answered prayers

Forgiveness

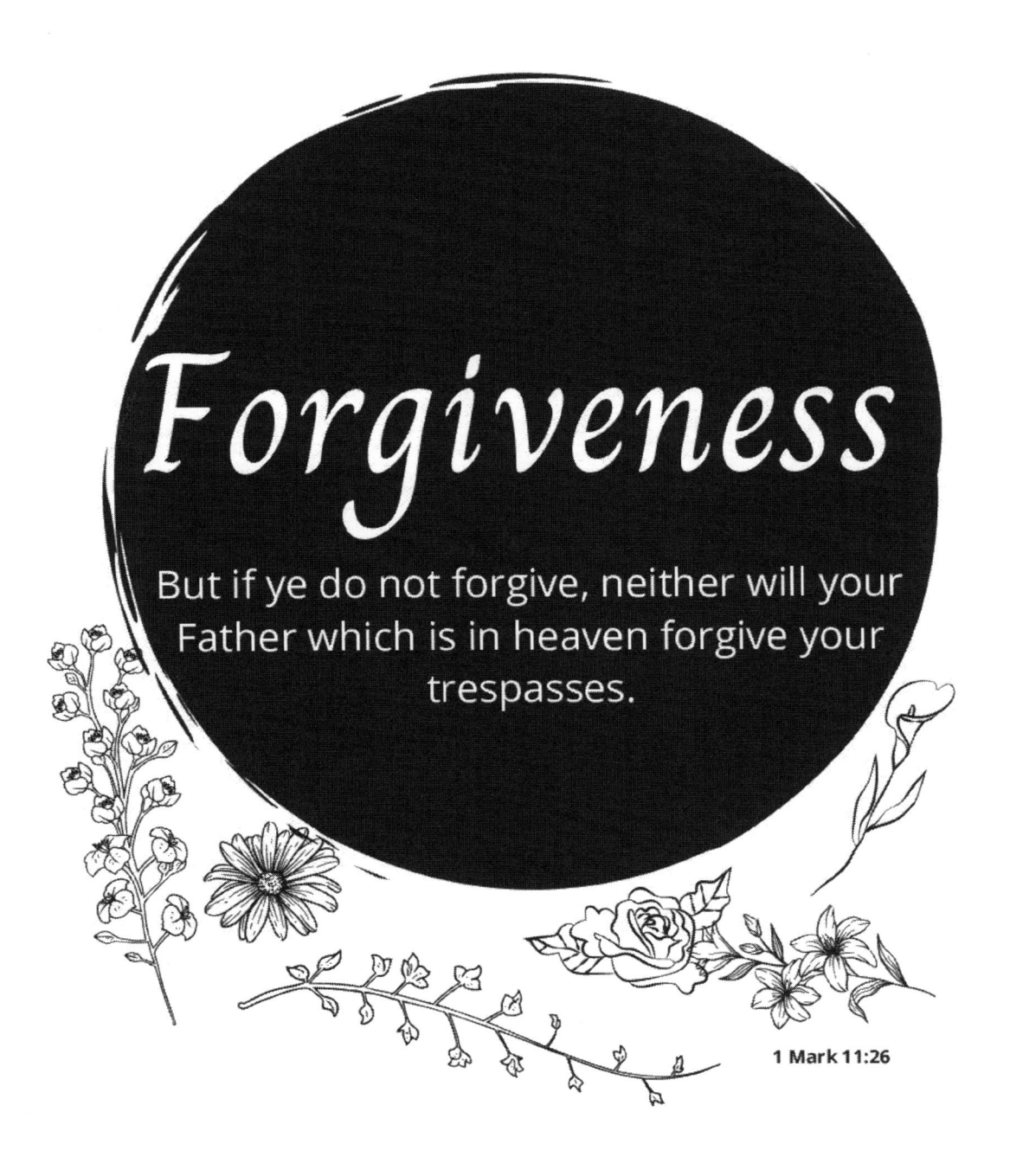

But if ye do not forgive, neither will your Father which is in heaven forgive your trespasses.

1 Mark 11:26

DATE:

Today's Bible Verse

Praise _____

Confessions:

Thankful for:

Prayer requests:

Answered Prayers

DATE:

Today's Bible Verse

Praise _____

Confessions:

Prayer requests:
_____
_____
_____
_____
_____
_____
_____
_____
_____

Thankful for:

Answered Prayers
_____
_____
_____
_____

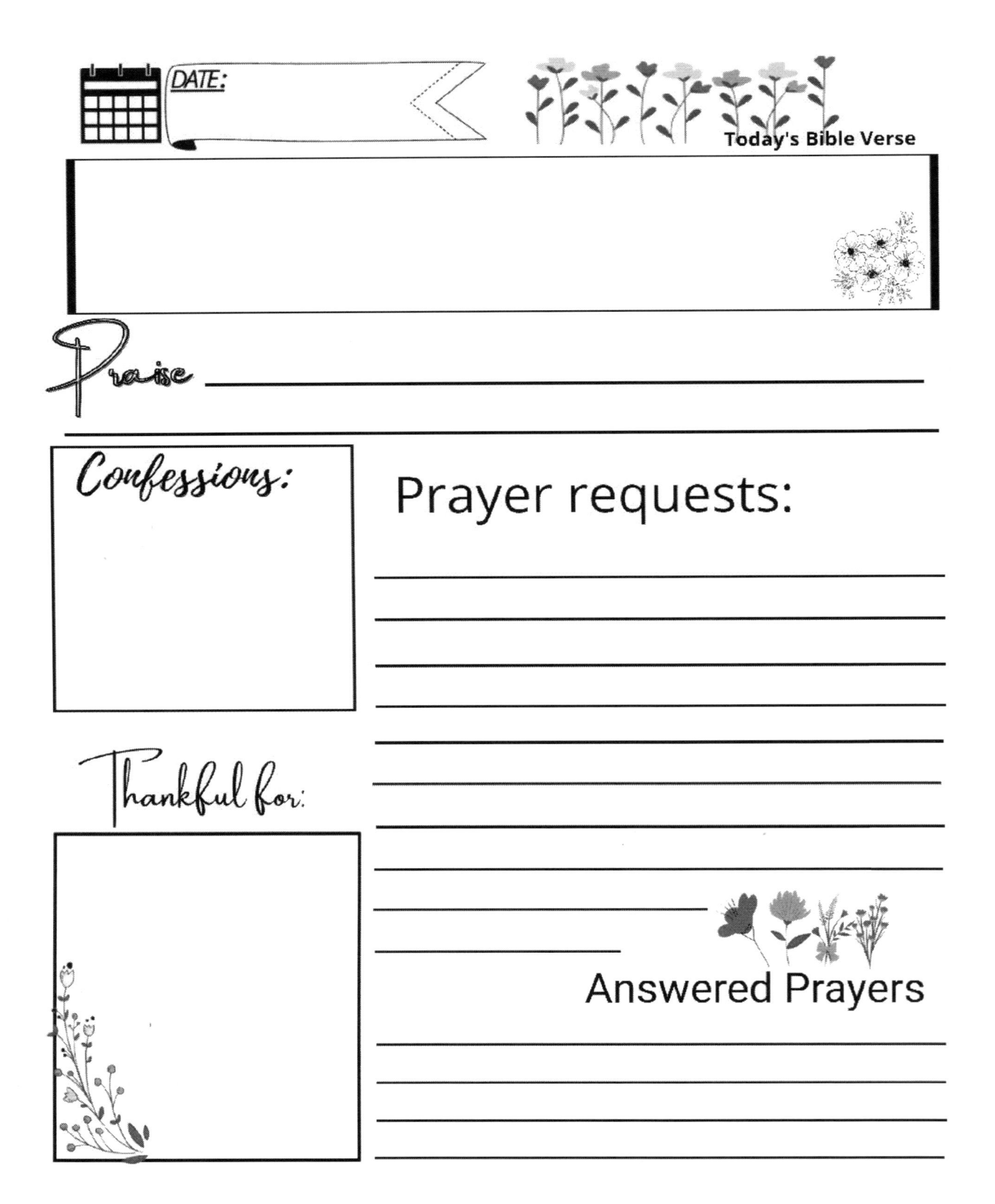

DATE:

Today's Bible Verse

Praise _____

Confessions:

Prayer requests:
_____
_____
_____
_____
_____
_____
_____
_____

Thankful for:

_____

Answered Prayers
_____
_____
_____
_____

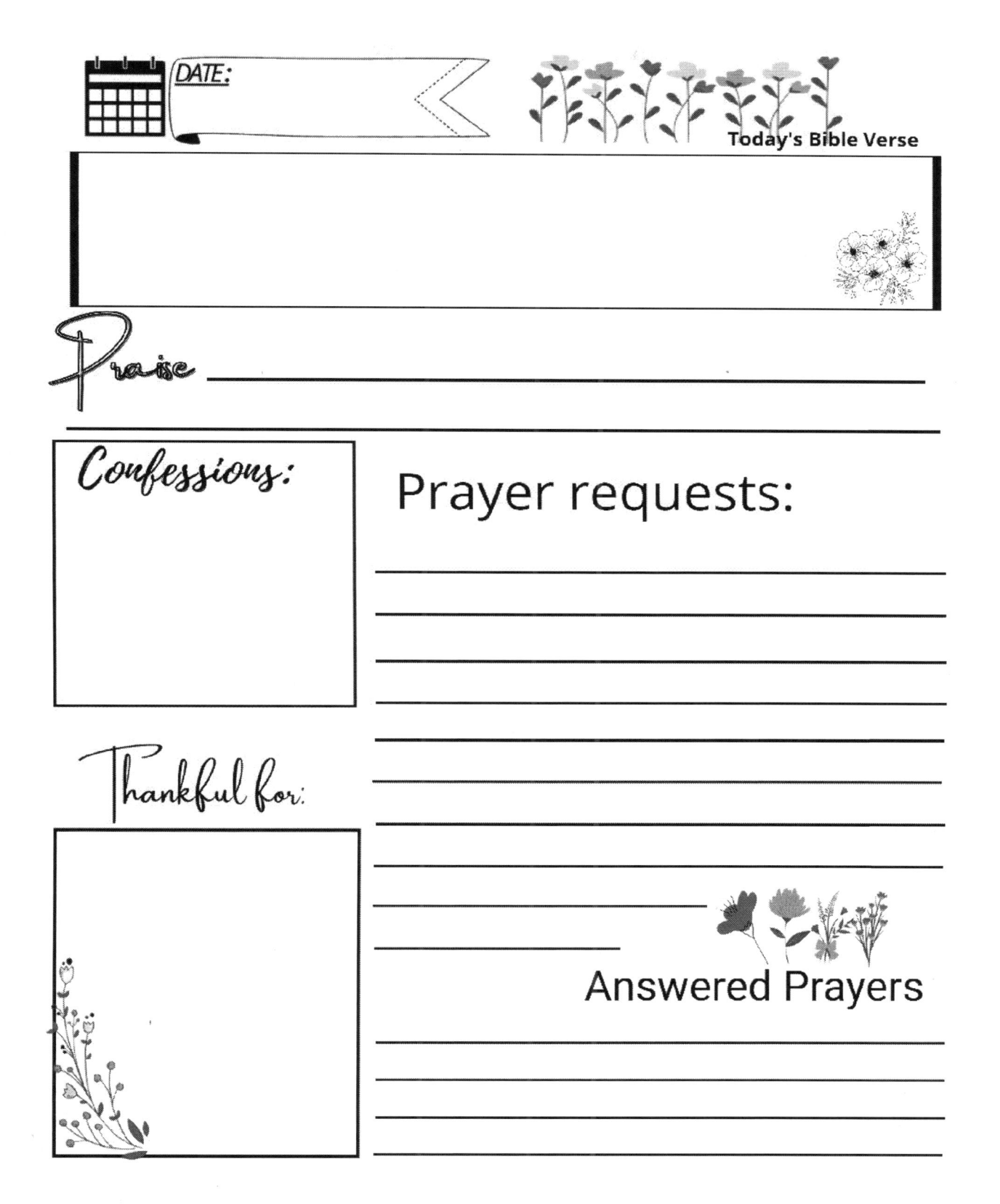

DATE:

Today's Bible Verse

Praise _____

Confessions:

Prayer requests:

_____
_____
_____
_____
_____
_____
_____
_____

Thankful for:

_____
_____

Answered Prayers

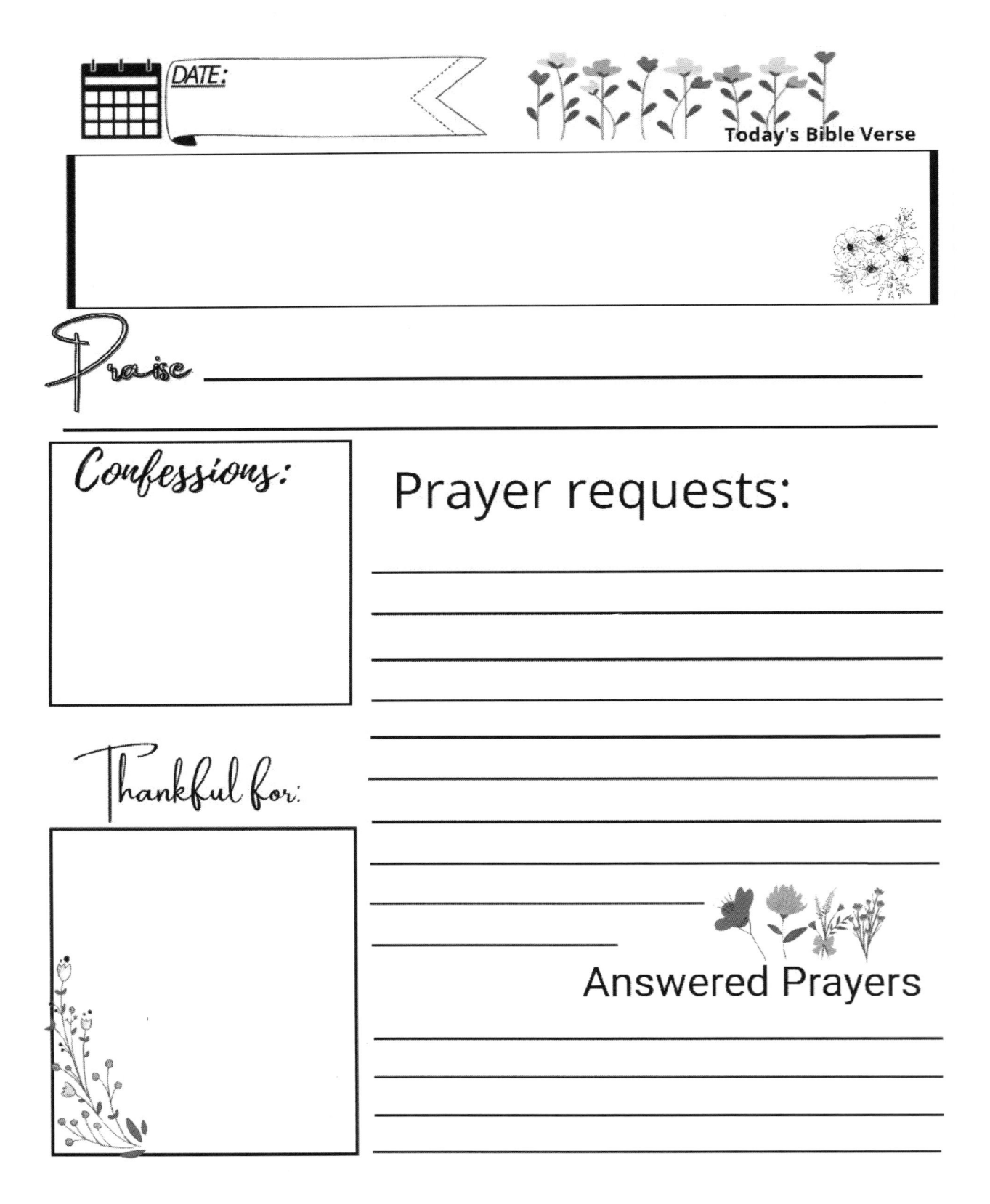

_____
_____
_____
_____

DATE:

Today's Bible Verse

Praise _____

Confessions:

Prayer requests:
_____
_____
_____
_____
_____
_____
_____
_____
_____

Thankful for:

Answered Prayers
_____
_____
_____
_____

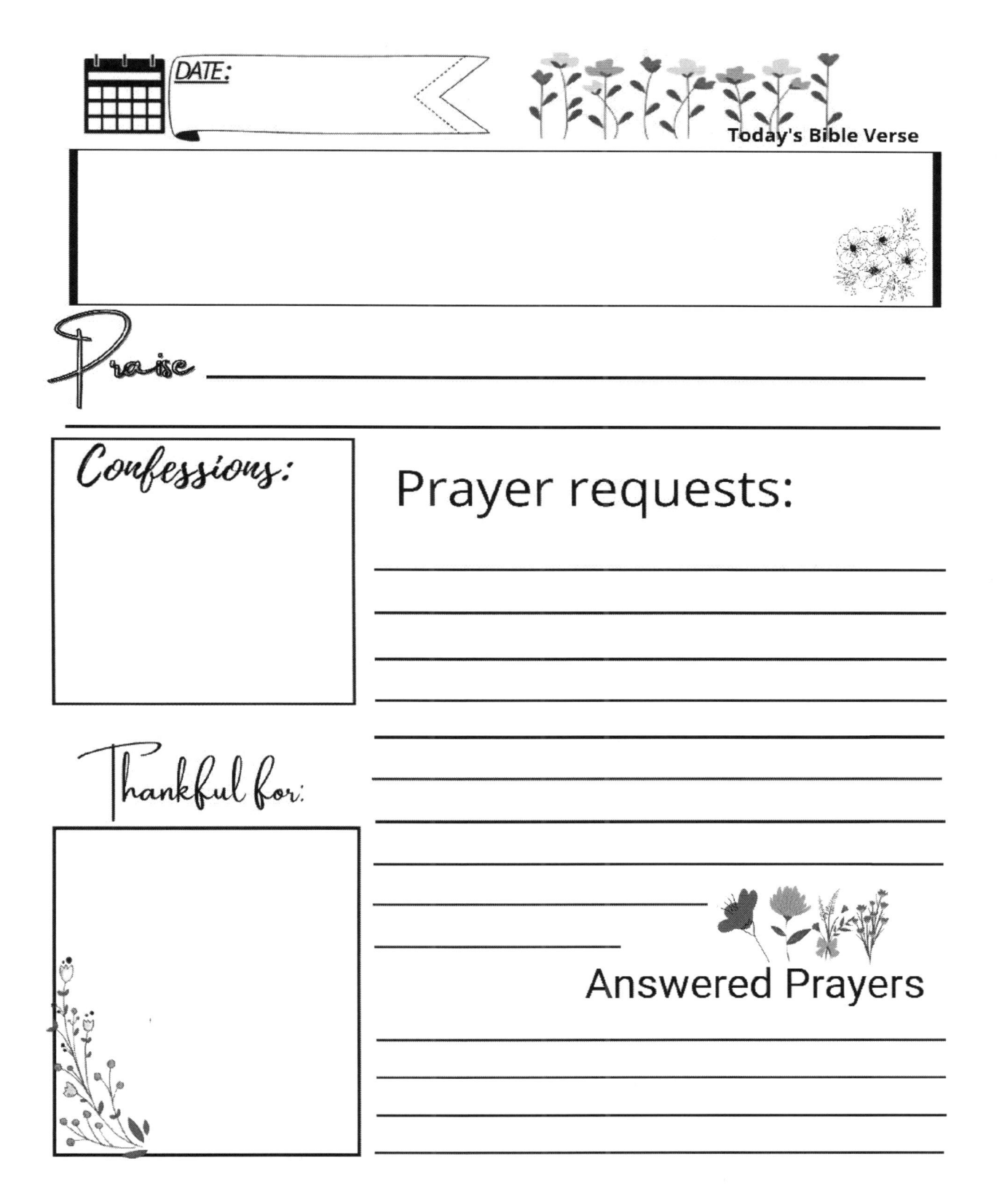

DATE:

Today's Bible Verse

Praise _____
_____

Confessions:

Thankful for:

Prayer requests:
_____
_____
_____
_____
_____
_____
_____
_____
_____
_____
_____

Answered Prayers
_____
_____
_____
_____

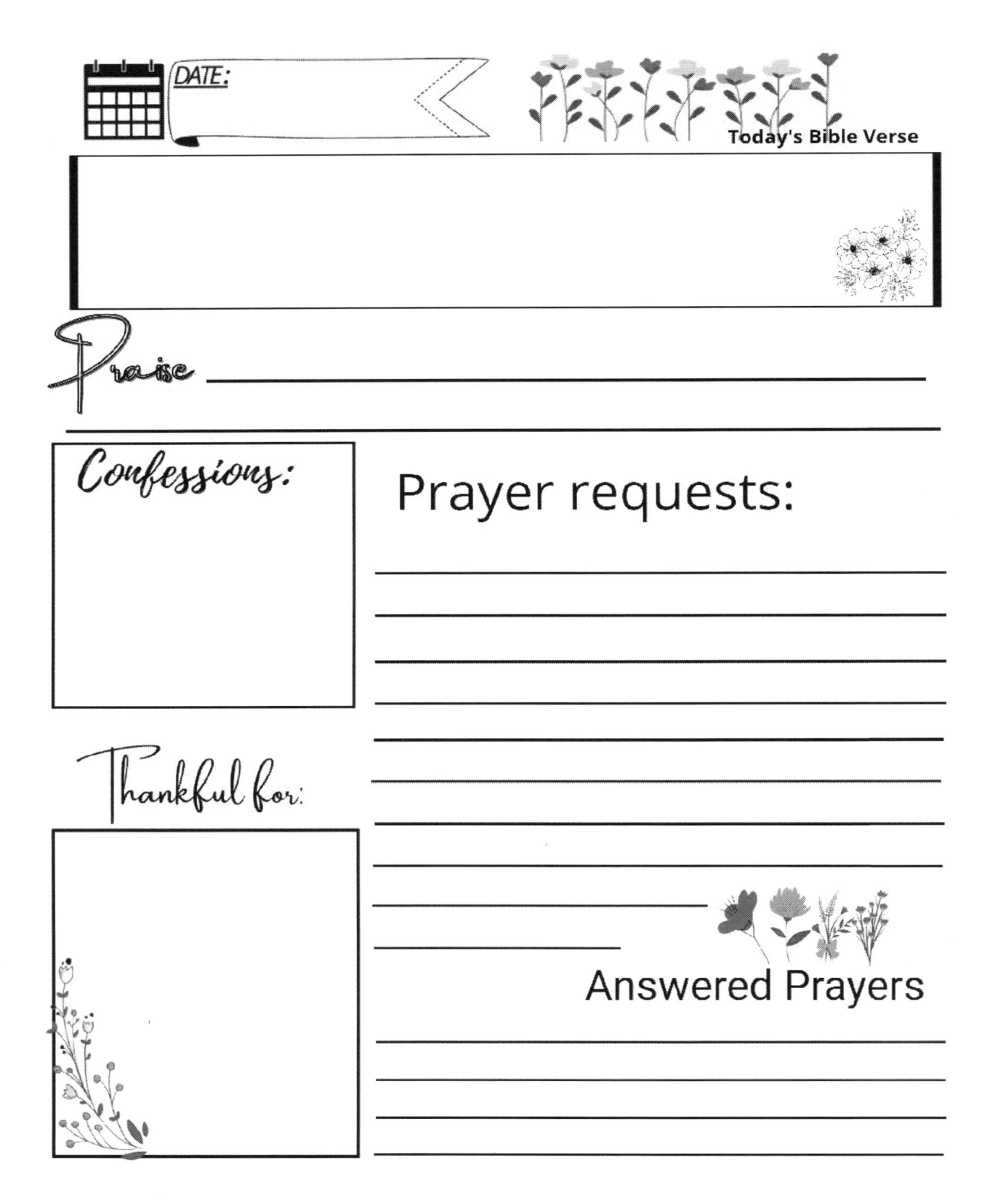

DATE:

Today's Bible Verse

Praise _____

Confessions:

Thankful for:

Prayer requests:

Answered Prayers

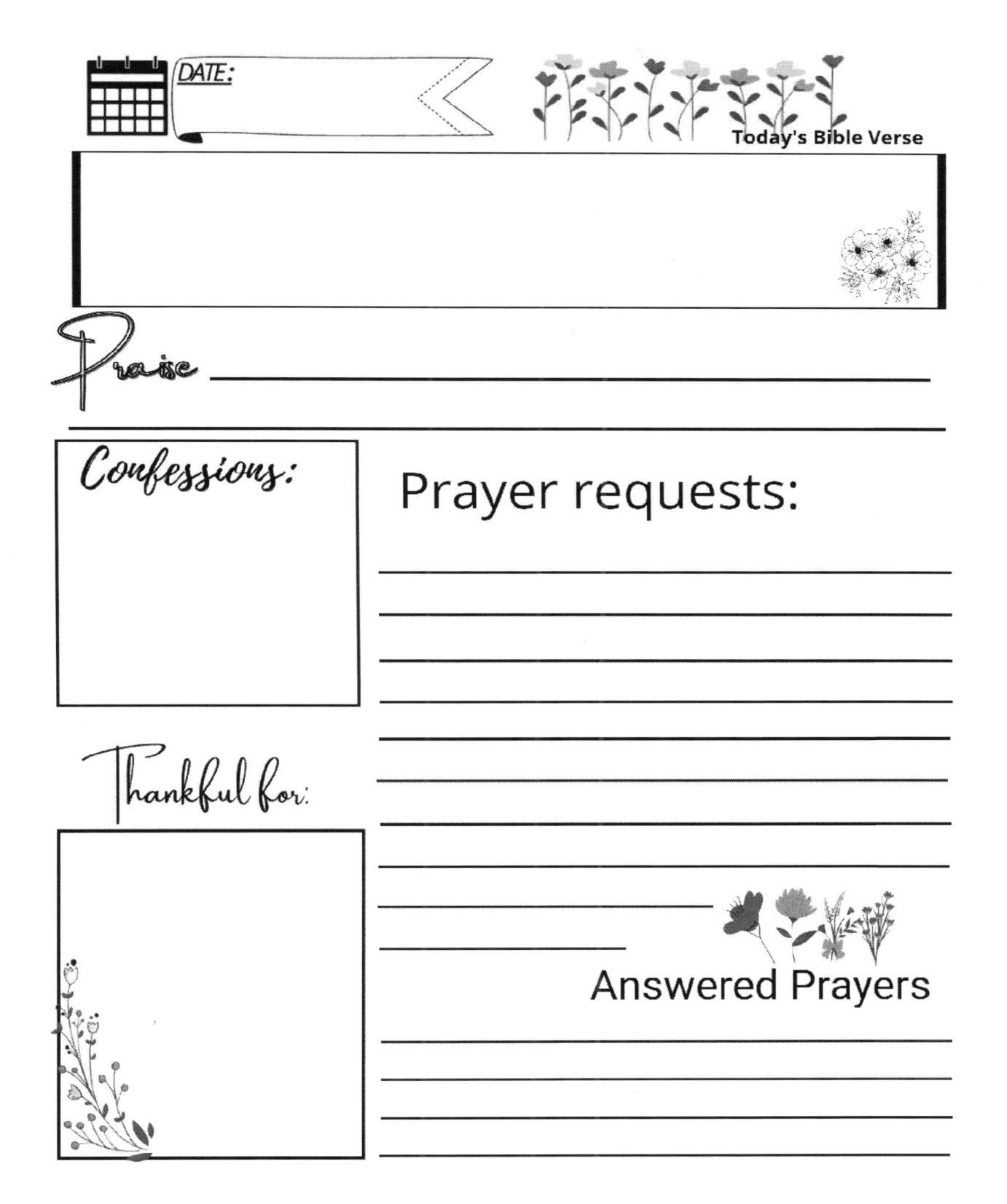

Related Chapter!

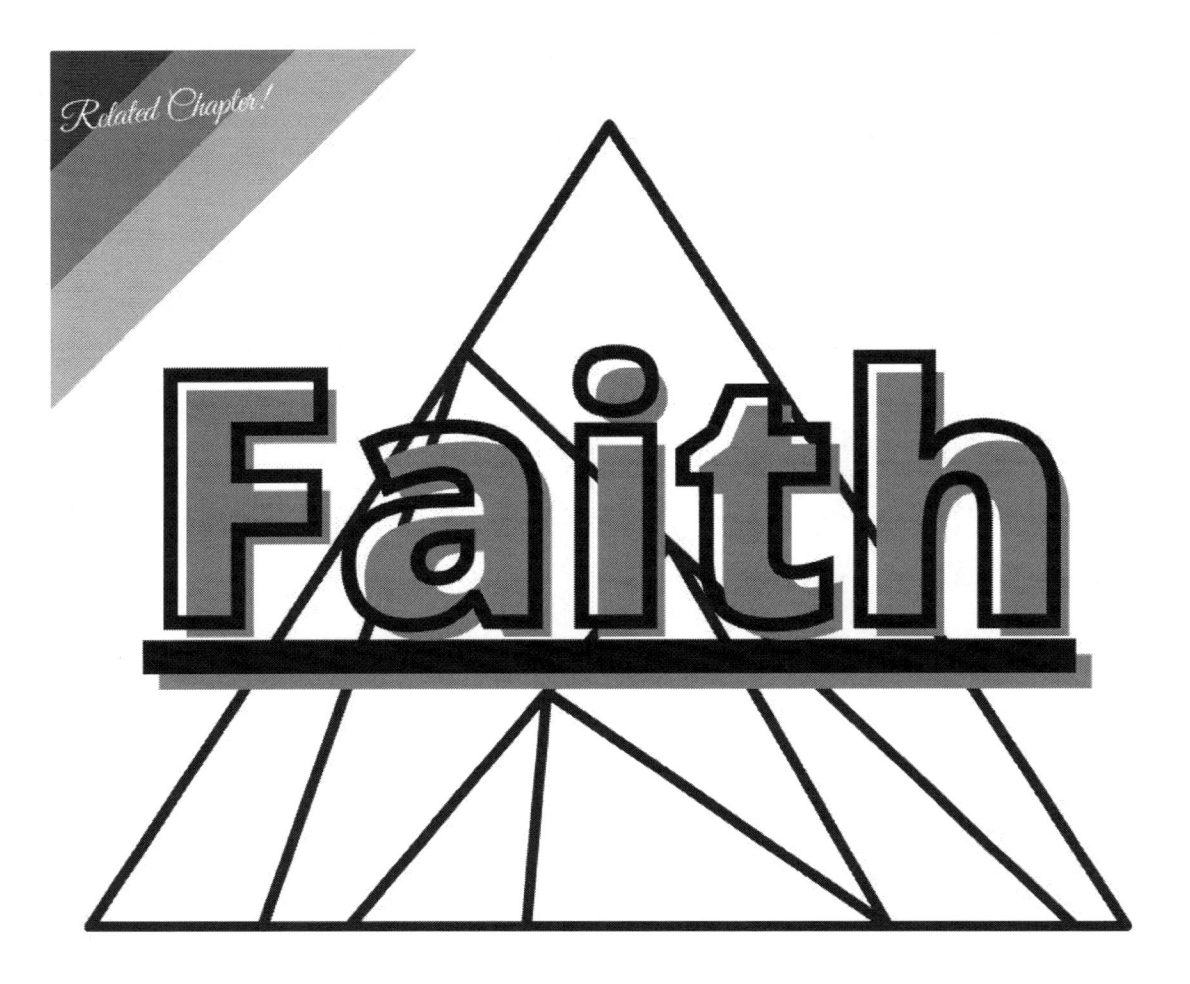

Faith

"For verily I say unto you, That whosoever shall say unto this mountain, Be thou removed, and be thou cast into the sea; and shall not doubt in his heart, but shall believe that those things which he saith shall come to pass; he shall have whatsoever he saith." —Mark 11:23

DATE:

Today's Bible Verse

Praise

Confessions:

Prayer requests:

Thankful for:

Answered prayers

DATE:

Today's Bible Verse

Praise _____

Confessions:

Thankful for:

Prayer requests:
_____
_____
_____
_____
_____
_____
_____
_____
_____

Answered prayers
_____
_____
_____
_____

DATE:

Today's Bible Verse

Praise _____

Confessions:

Prayer requests:

Thankful for:

Answered prayers

DATE:

Today's Bible Verse

Praise _____

Confessions:

Prayer requests:

Thankful for:

Answered prayers

DATE:

Today's Bible Verse

Praise _____

Confessions:

Prayer requests:
_____
_____
_____
_____
_____
_____
_____
_____
_____
_____

Thankful for:

Answered prayers
_____
_____
_____
_____

DATE:

Today's Bible Verse

Praise _____

Confessions:

Prayer requests:

Thankful for:

Answered prayers

DATE:

Today's Bible Verse

Praise _____

Confessions:

Prayer requests:

Thankful for:

Answered prayers

Goodness & Mercy

6 Surely goodness and mercy shall follow me all the days of my life: and I will dwell in the house of the Lord for ever.

Psalm 23:6

DATE:

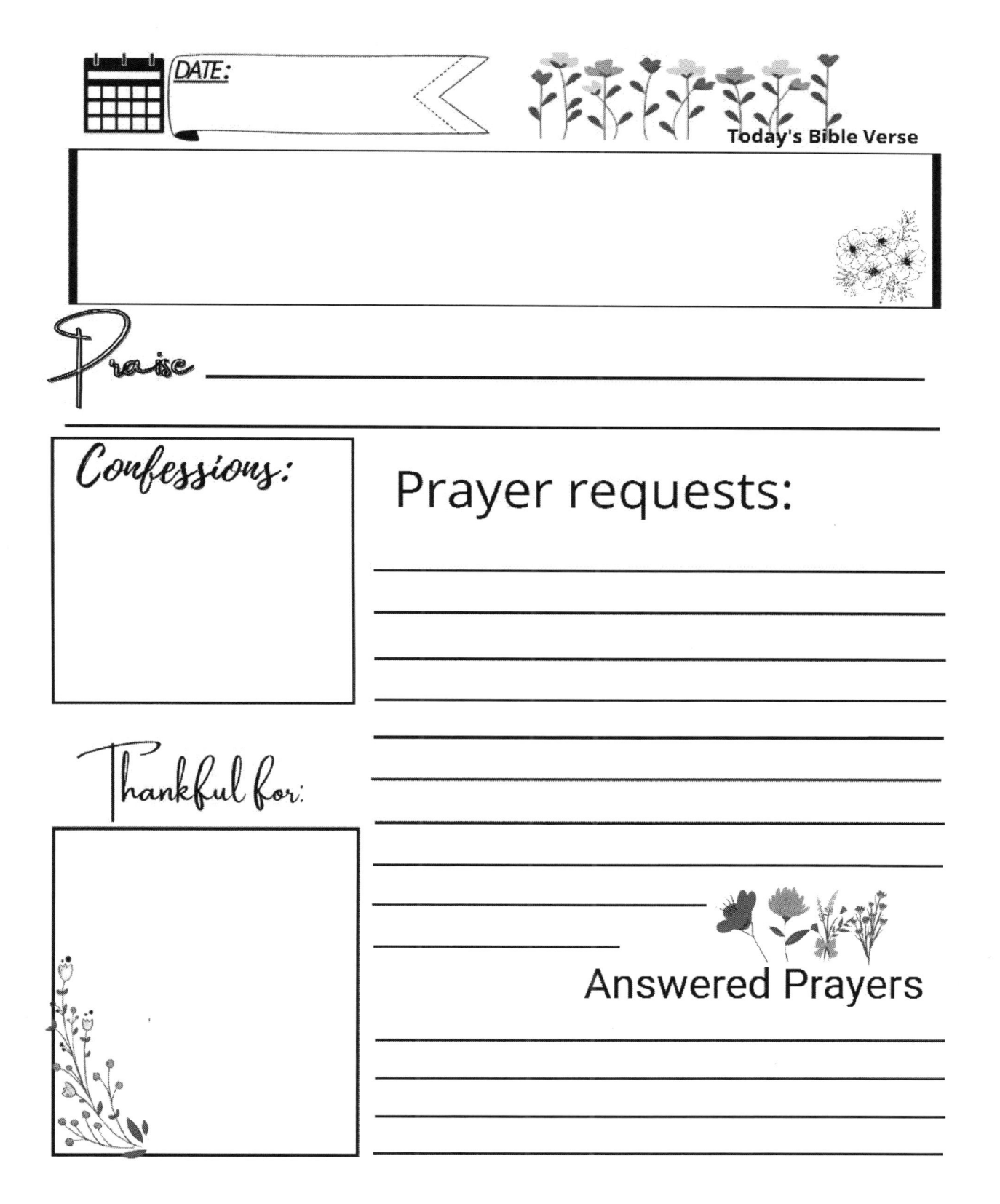

Today's Bible Verse

Praise _____

Confessions:

Prayer requests:

Thankful for:

Answered Prayers

DATE:

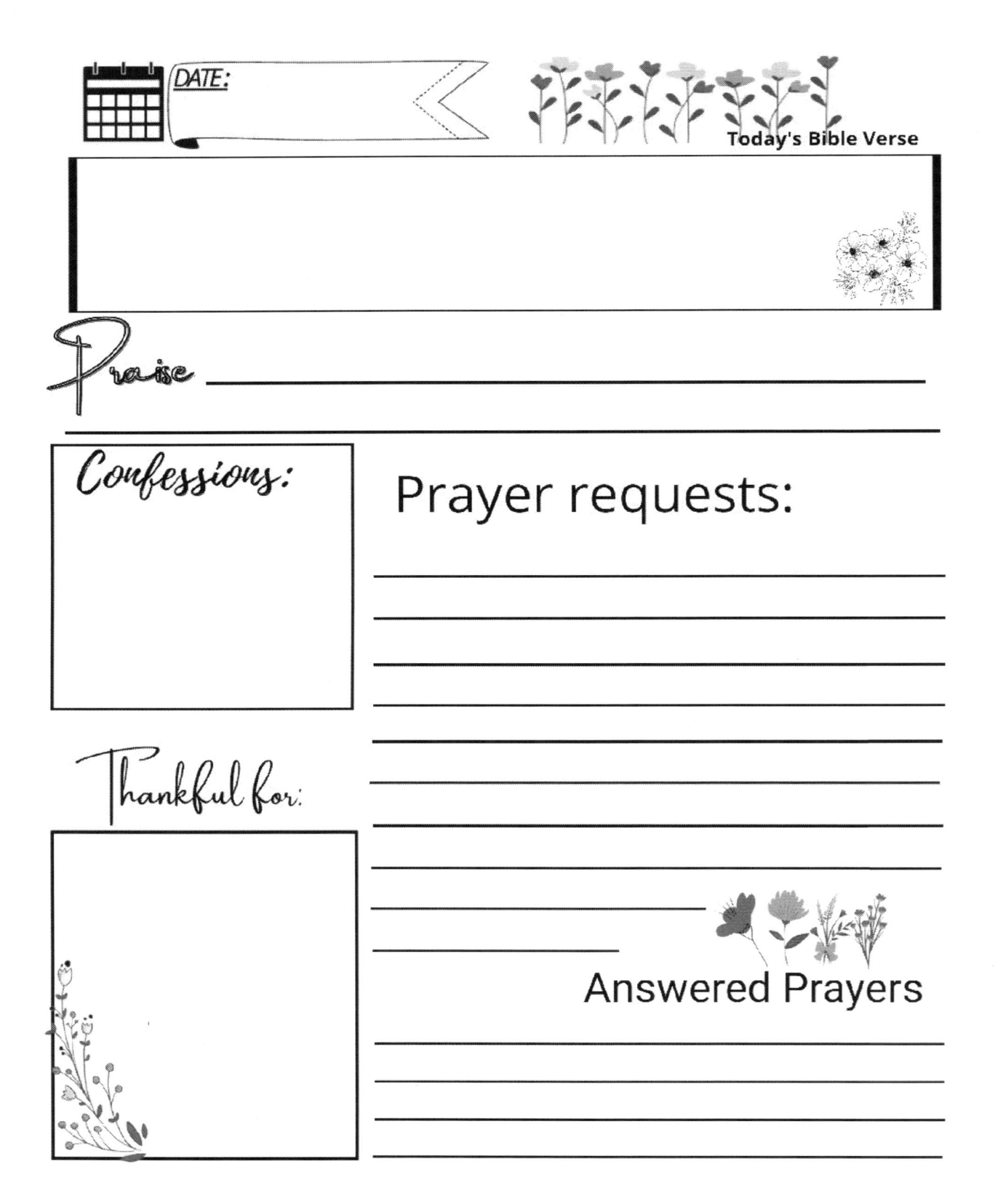

Today's Bible Verse

Praise _____

Confessions:

Thankful for:

Prayer requests:

_____
_____
_____
_____
_____
_____
_____
_____
_____

Answered Prayers

_____
_____
_____
_____

DATE:

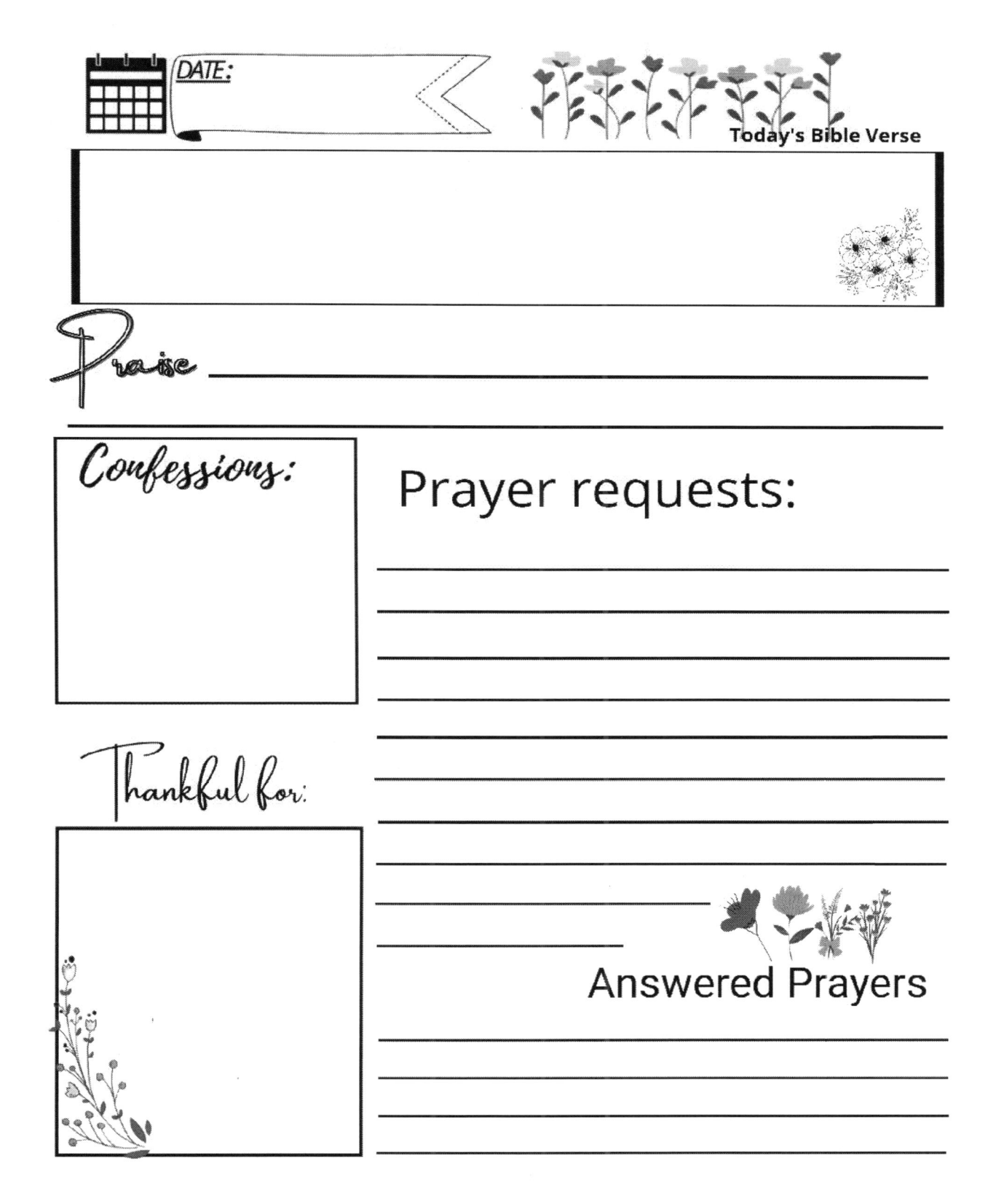

Today's Bible Verse

Praise _____

Confessions:

Prayer requests:

Thankful for:

Answered Prayers

DATE:

Today's Bible Verse

Praise _____

Confessions:

Prayer requests:
_____
_____
_____
_____
_____
_____
_____

Thankful for:

_____

Answered Prayers
_____
_____
_____
_____

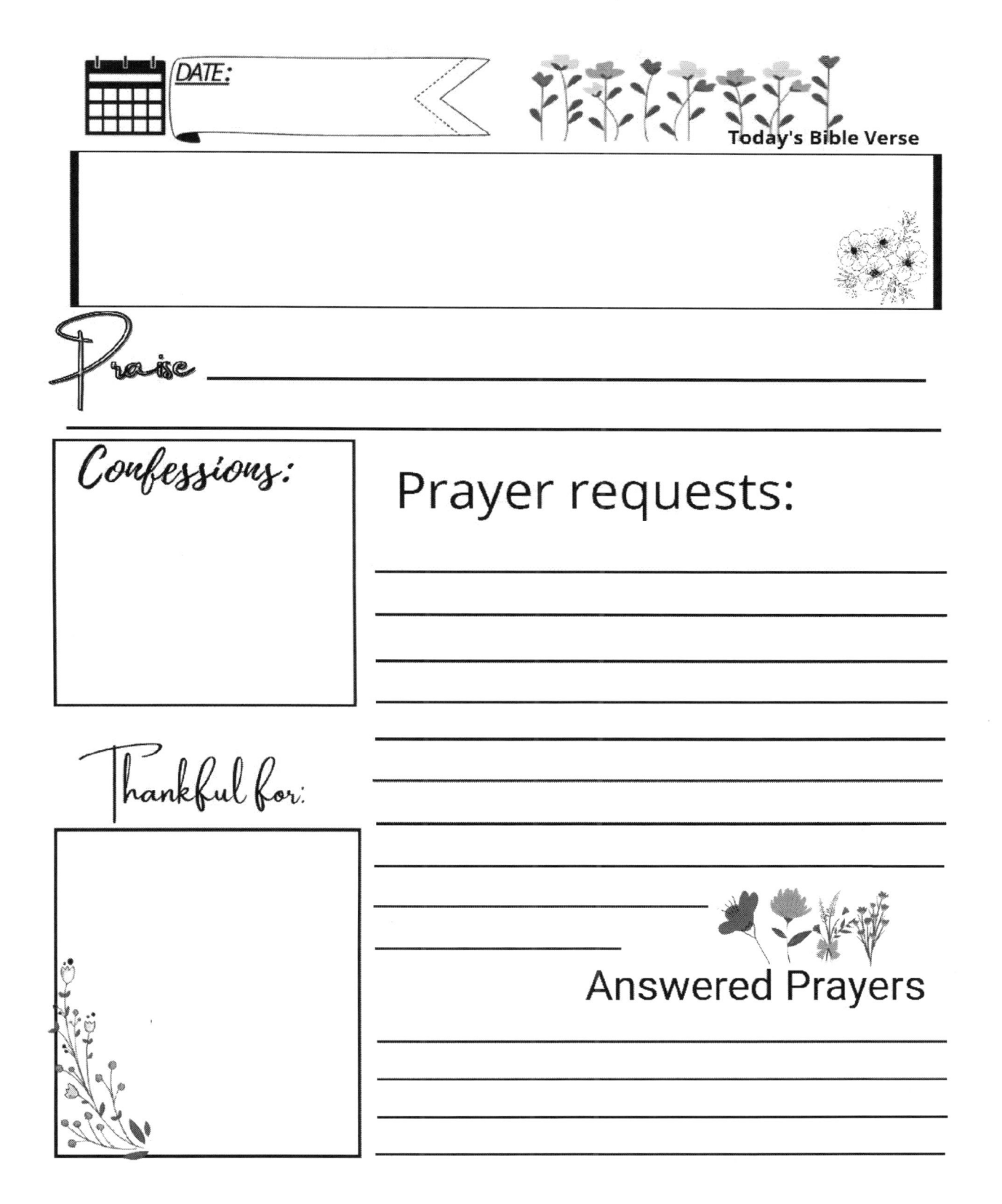

DATE:

Today's Bible Verse

Praise _____

Confessions:

Prayer requests:
_____
_____
_____
_____
_____
_____
_____
_____

Thankful for:

_____

Answered Prayers
_____
_____
_____
_____

DATE:

Today's Bible Verse

Praise _____

Confessions:

Prayer requests:

_____
_____
_____
_____
_____
_____
_____
_____

Thankful for:

Answered Prayers

_____
_____
_____
_____

DATE:

Today's Bible Verse

Praise _____

Confessions:

Prayer requests:
_____
_____
_____
_____
_____
_____

Thankful for:

_____
_____
_____

Answered Prayers

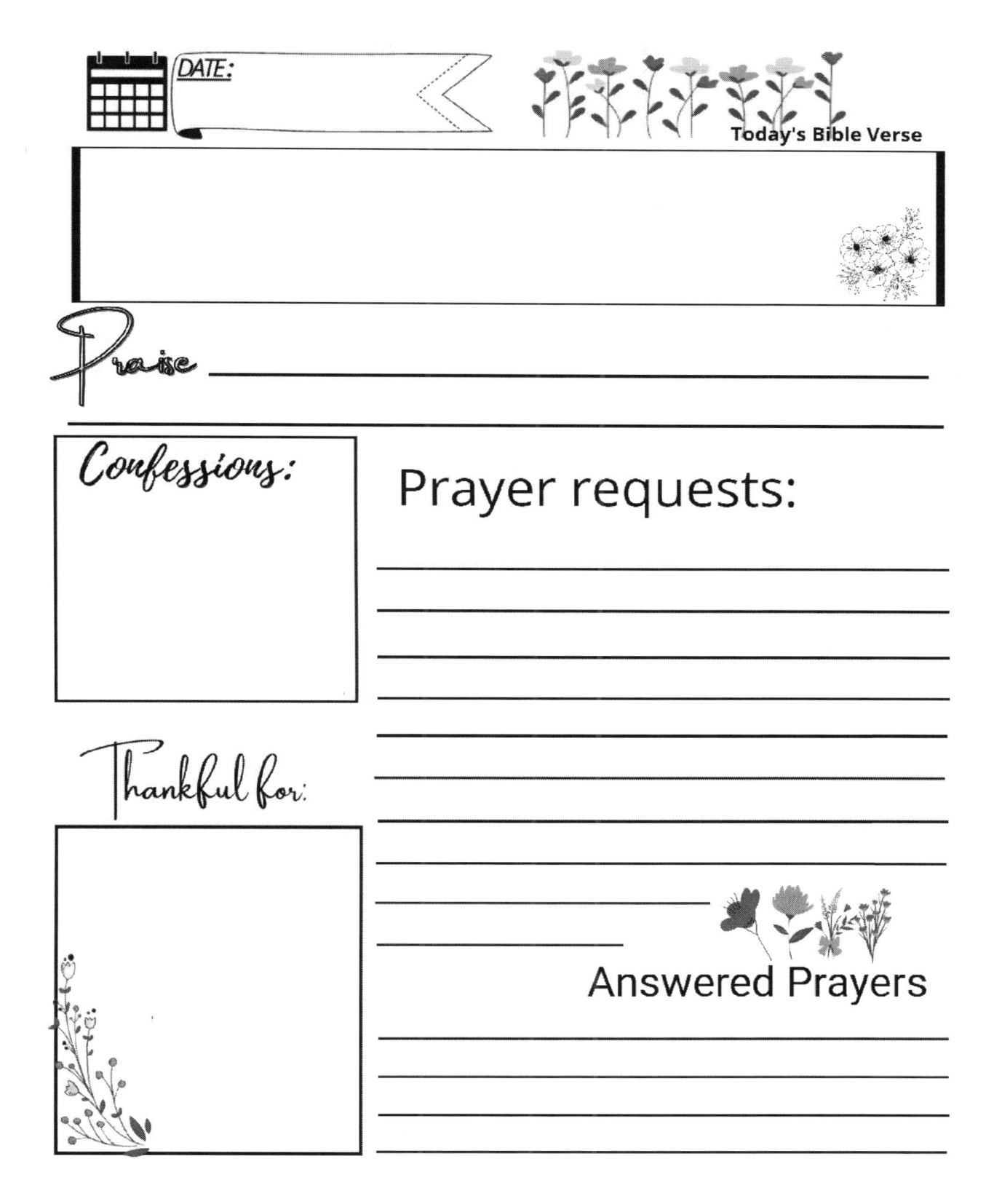

_____
_____
_____
_____

With God, all things are possible!

26 But Jesus beheld them, and said unto them, With men this is impossible; but with God all things are possible.

Mark 19:26

20 And Jesus said unto them, Because of your unbelief: for verily I say unto you, If ye have faith as a grain of mustard seed, ye shall say unto this mountain, Remove hence to yonder place; and it shall remove; and nothing shall be impossible unto you.

Matthew 17:20

DATE:

Today's Bible Verse

Praise

Confessions:

Prayer requests:

Thankful for:

Answered prayers

DATE:

Today's Bible Verse

Praise _____

Confessions:

Prayer requests:
_____
_____
_____
_____
_____
_____
_____

Thankful for:

_____
_____

Answered prayers
_____
_____
_____
_____

DATE:

Today's Bible Verse

Praise _____

Confessions:

Prayer requests:
_____
_____
_____
_____
_____
_____
_____
_____

Thankful for:

_____

Answered prayers
_____
_____
_____
_____

DATE:

Today's Bible Verse

Praise _____

Confessions:

Prayer requests:
_____
_____
_____
_____
_____
_____
_____

Thankful for:

_____

Answered prayers
_____
_____
_____
_____

DATE:

Today's Bible Verse

Praise

Confessions:

Prayer requests:

Thankful for:

Answered prayers

DATE:

Today's Bible Verse

Praise

Confessions:

Prayer requests:

Thankful for:

Answered prayers

DATE:

Today's Bible Verse

Praise _____

Confessions:

Prayer requests:

Thankful for:

Answered prayers

Wealth

4 By humility and the fear of the Lord are riches, and honour, and life.

Proverbs 22:4

18 But thou shalt remember the Lord thy God: for it is he that giveth thee power to get wealth, that he may establish his covenant which he sware unto thy fathers, as it is this day.

Deuteronomy 8:18

DATE:

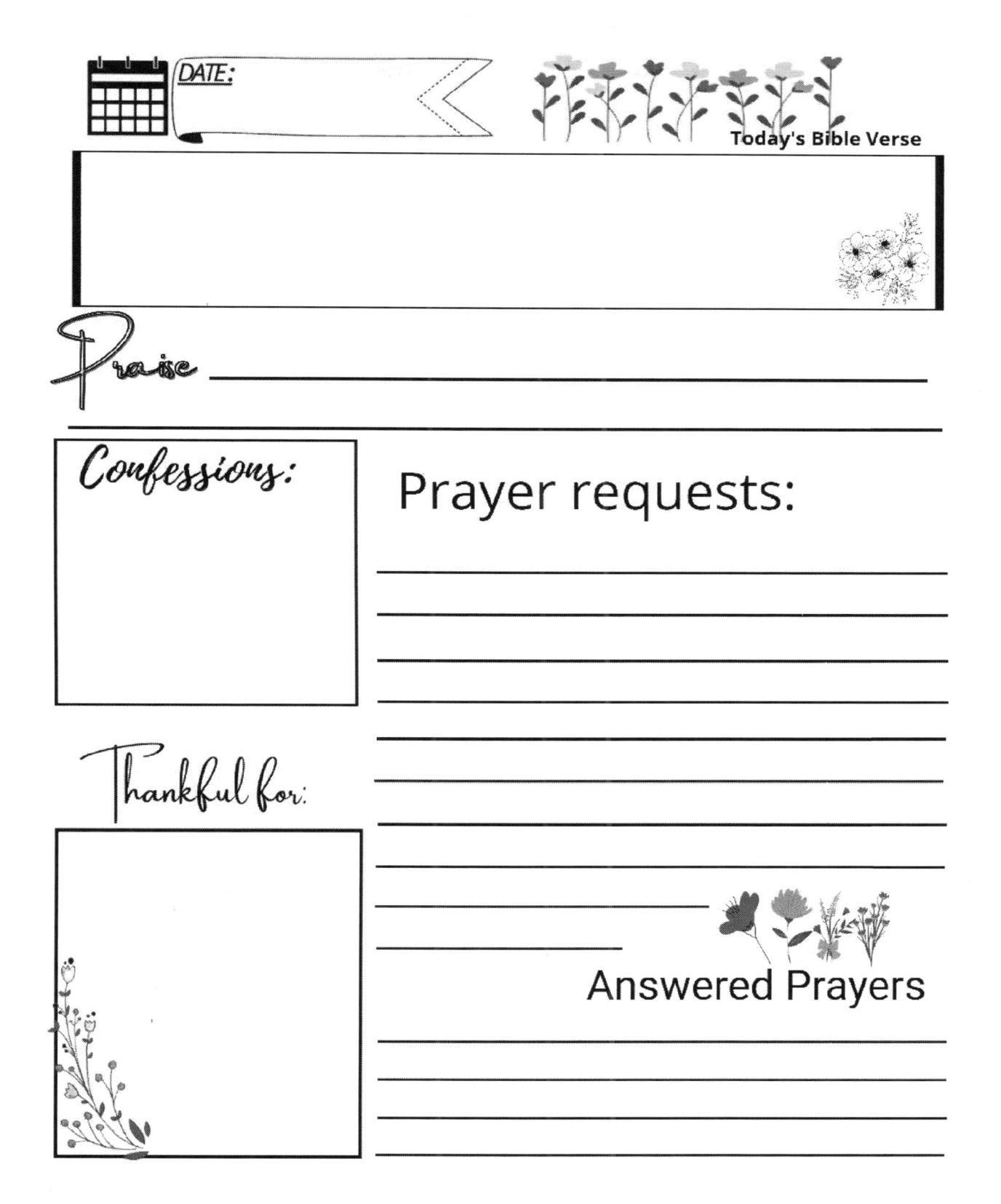

Today's Bible Verse

Praise _____

Confessions:

Prayer requests:

Thankful for:

Answered Prayers

DATE:

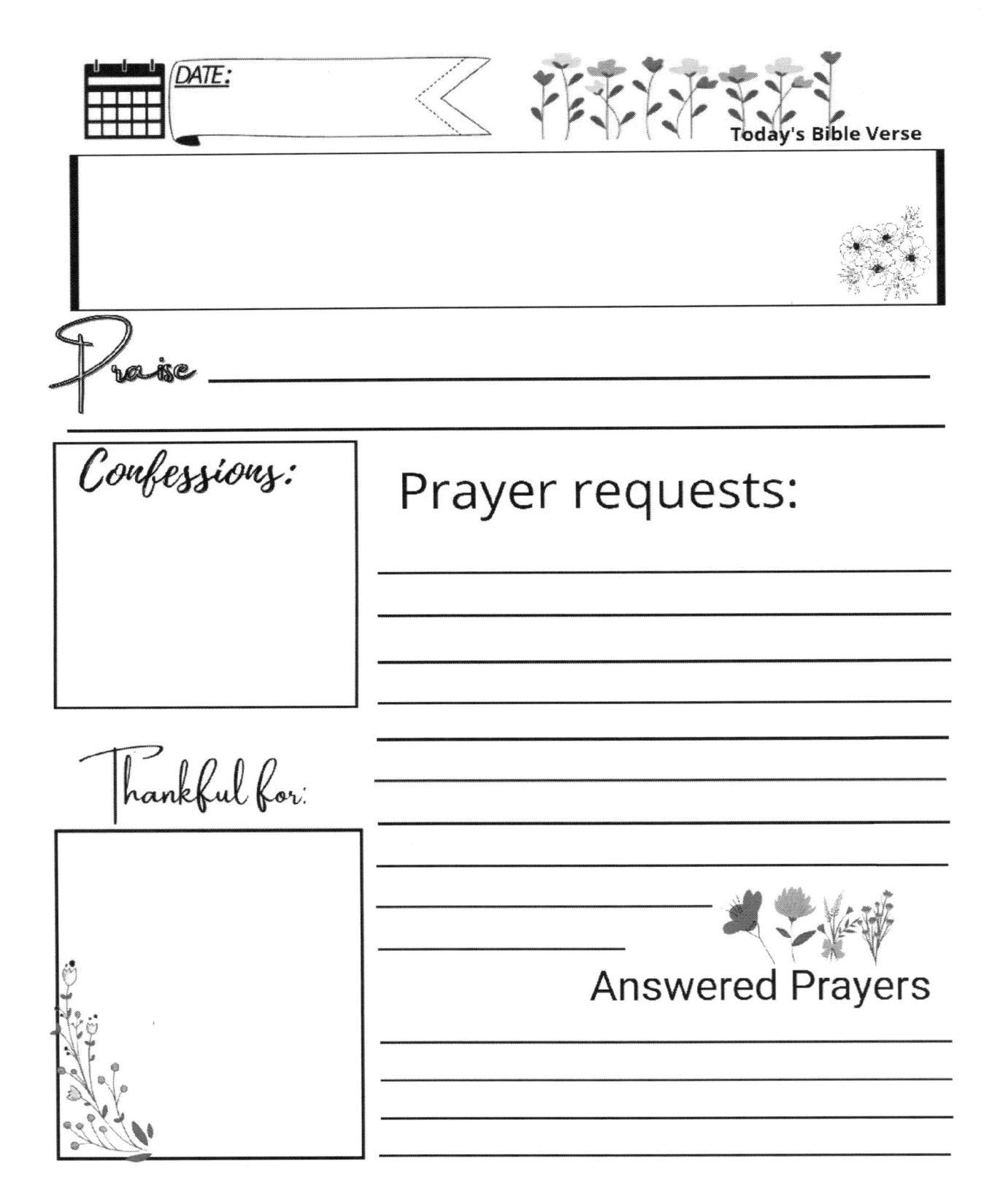

Today's Bible Verse

Praise _____

Confessions:

Prayer requests:

Thankful for:

Answered Prayers

DATE:

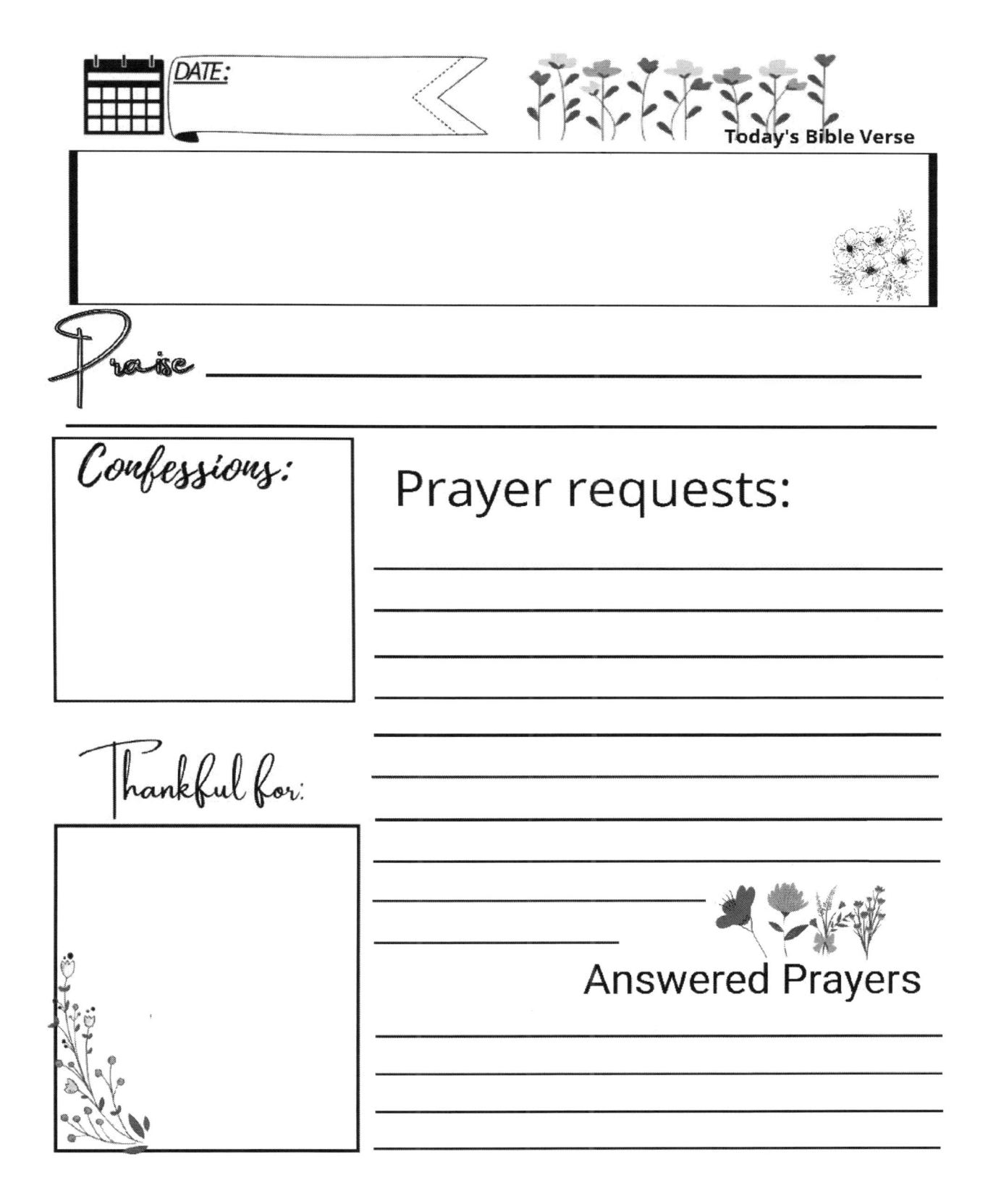

Today's Bible Verse

Praise _____

Confessions:

Thankful for:

Prayer requests:

_____
_____
_____
_____
_____
_____
_____
_____
_____

Answered Prayers

_____
_____
_____
_____

DATE:

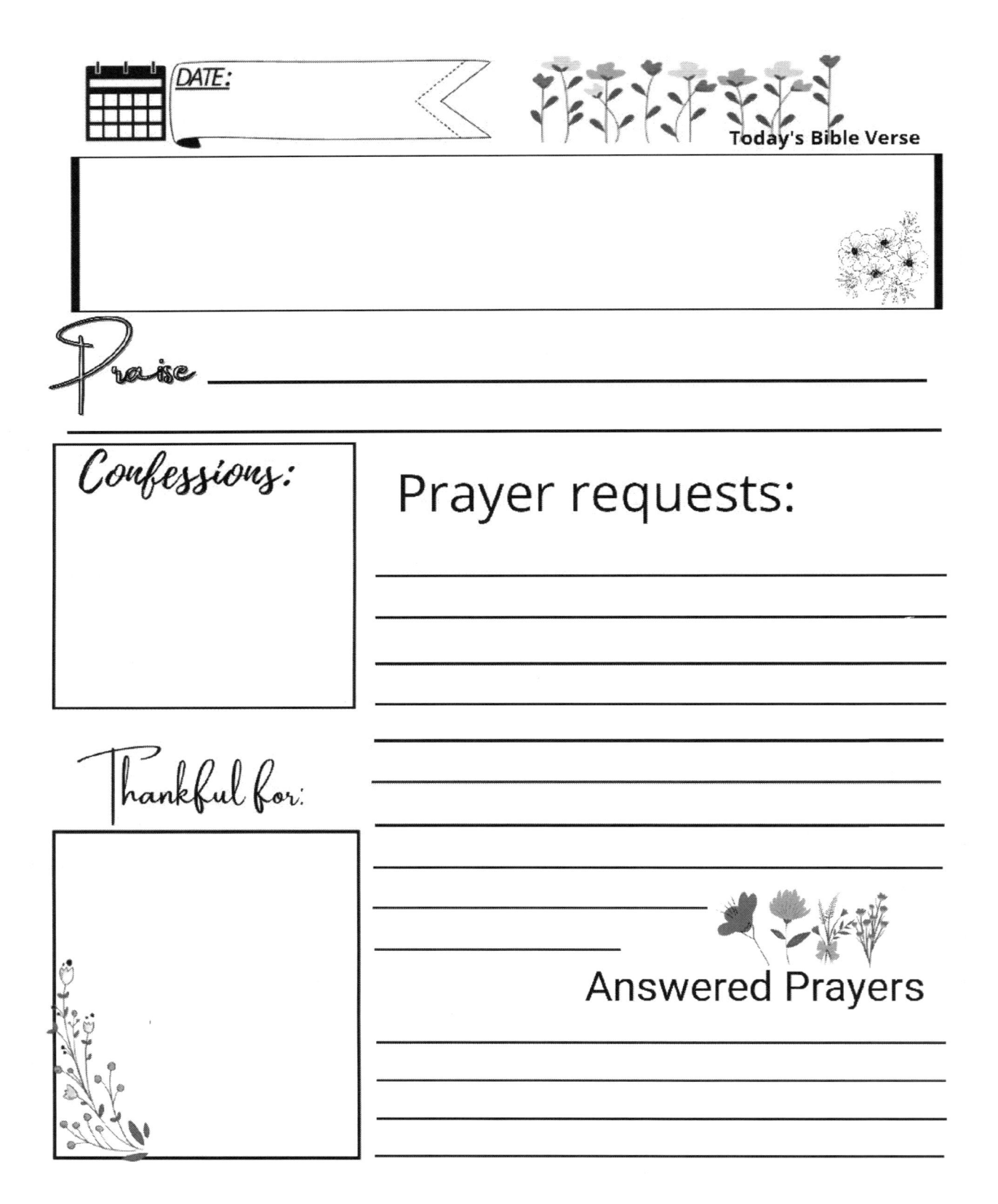

Today's Bible Verse

Praise _____

Confessions:

Prayer requests:

Thankful for:

Answered Prayers

DATE:

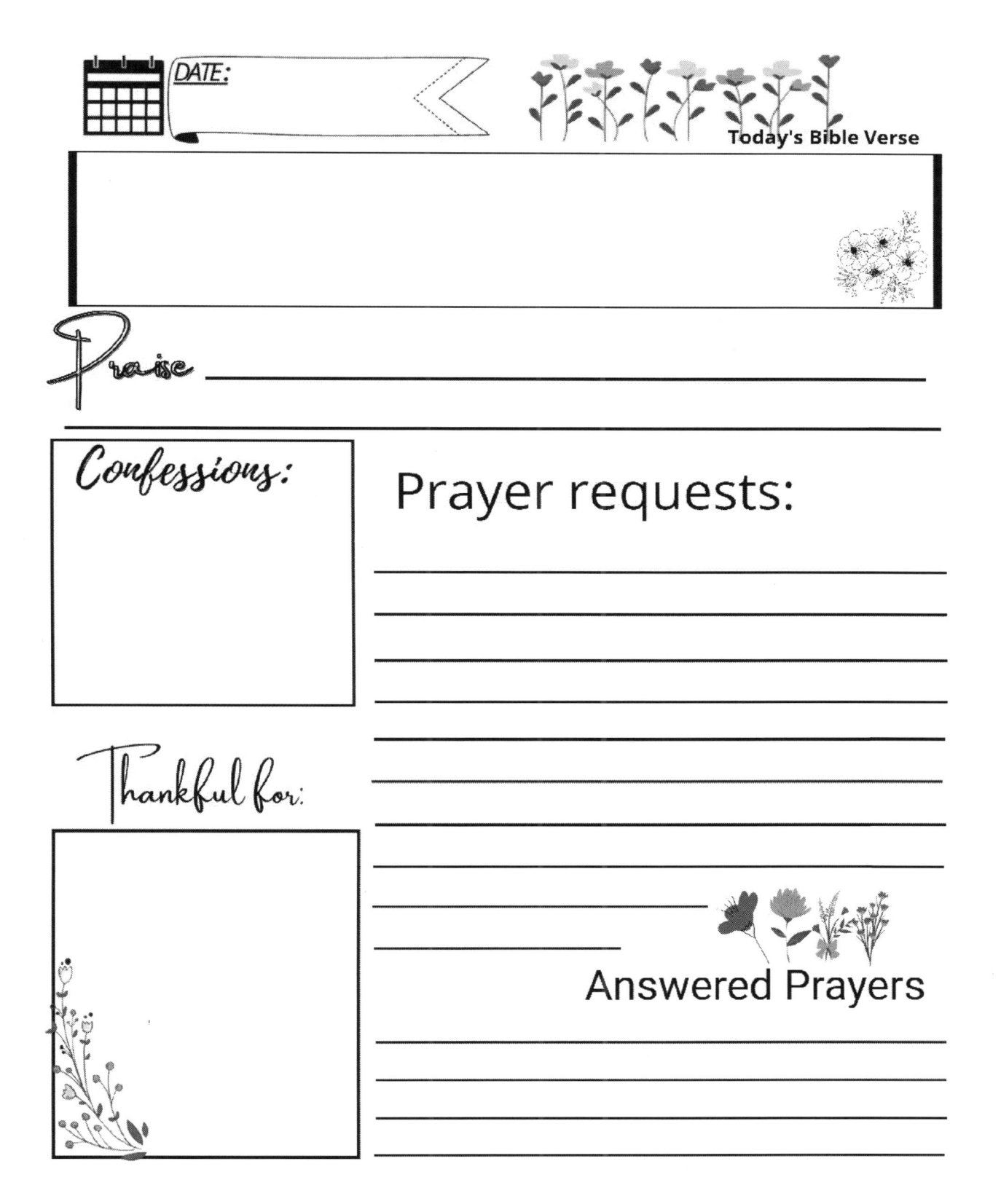

Today's Bible Verse

Praise _____

Confessions:

Prayer requests:
_____
_____
_____
_____
_____
_____
_____
_____

Thankful for:

Answered Prayers
_____
_____
_____
_____

DATE:

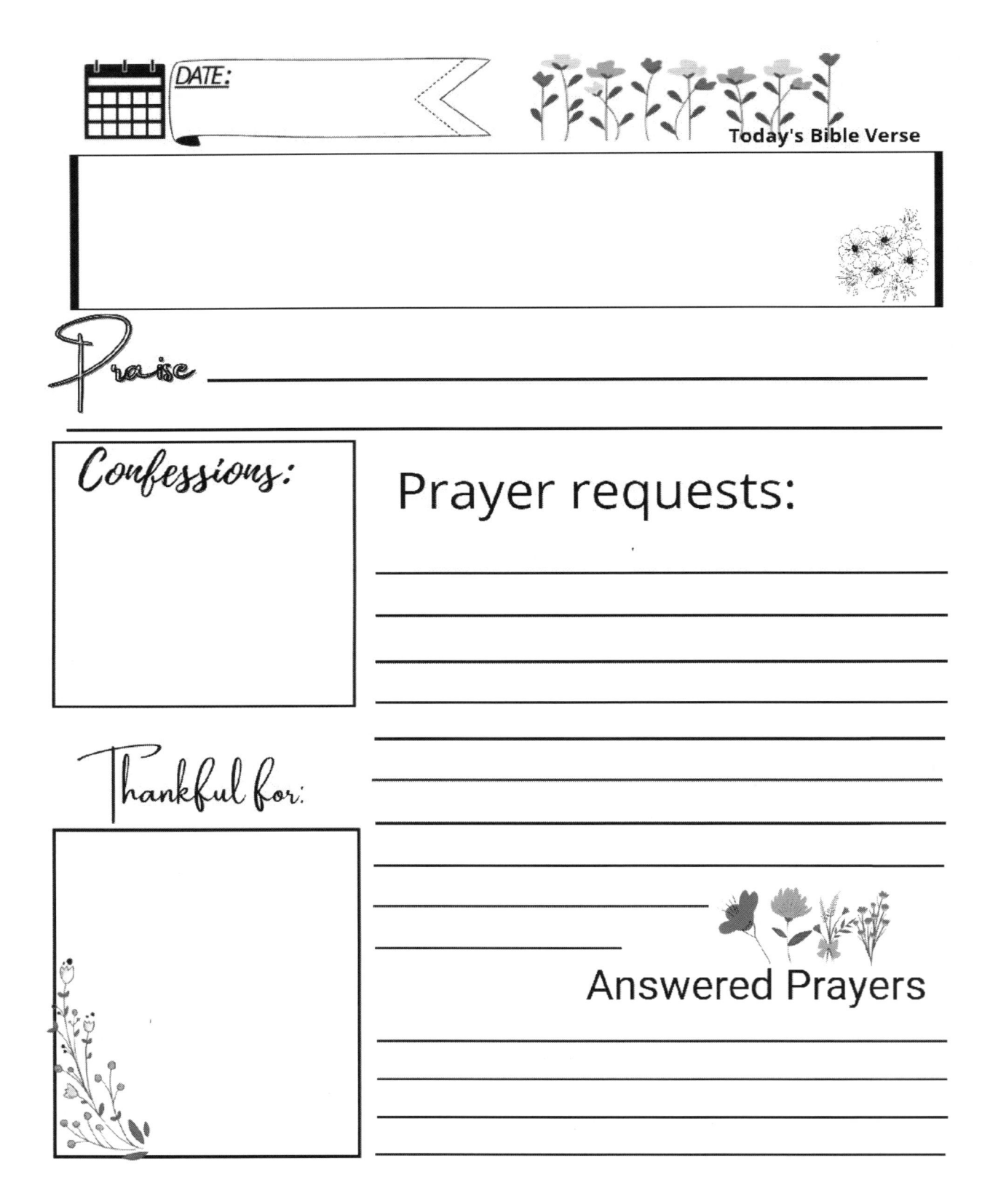

Today's Bible Verse

Praise _____

Confessions:

Prayer requests:
_____
_____
_____
_____
_____
_____
_____
_____

Thankful for:

_____
_____

Answered Prayers
_____
_____
_____
_____

DATE:

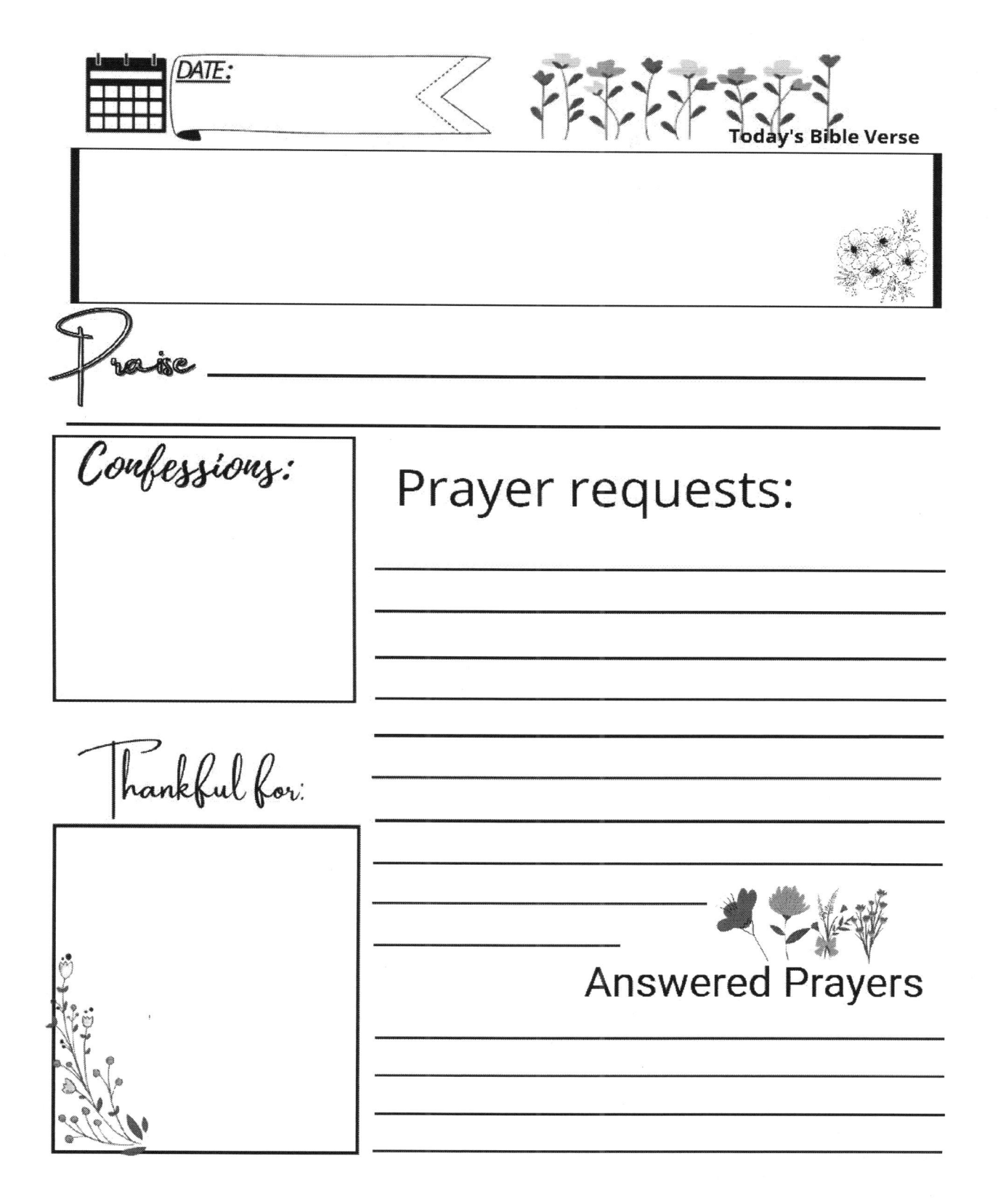

Today's Bible Verse

Praise _____

Confessions:

Prayer requests:

_____
_____
_____
_____
_____
_____
_____

Thankful for:

_____
_____

Answered Prayers

_____
_____
_____
_____

Rest & Peace

28 Come unto me, all ye that labour and are heavy laden, and I will give you rest.
29 Take my yoke upon you, and learn of me; for I am meek and lowly in heart: and ye shall find rest unto your souls.
30 For my yoke is easy, and my burden is light.

- Matthew 11:28-30

DATE:

Today's Bible Verse

Praise _____

Confessions:

Prayer requests:
_____
_____
_____
_____
_____
_____
_____
_____
_____
_____
_____

Thankful for:

Answered prayers
_____
_____
_____
_____

DATE:

Today's Bible Verse

Praise _____

Confessions:

Prayer requests:

Thankful for:

Answered prayers

DATE:

Today's Bible Verse

Praise _____

Confessions:

Thankful for:

Prayer requests:

Answered prayers

DATE:

Today's Bible Verse

Praise _____

Confessions:

Prayer requests:

Thankful for:

Answered prayers

DATE:

Today's Bible Verse

Praise _____

Confessions:

Thankful for:

Prayer requests:
_____
_____
_____
_____
_____
_____
_____
_____
_____
_____

Answered prayers
_____
_____
_____
_____

DATE:

Today's Bible Verse

Praise _____

Confessions:

Prayer requests:

Thankful for:

Answered prayers

DATE:

Today's Bible Verse

Praise

Confessions:

Prayer requests:

Thankful for:

Answered prayers

Healing and wholeness

5 But he was wounded for our transgressions, he was bruised for our iniquities: the chastisement of our peace was upon him; and with his stripes we are healed.

- Isaiah 53:5

DATE:

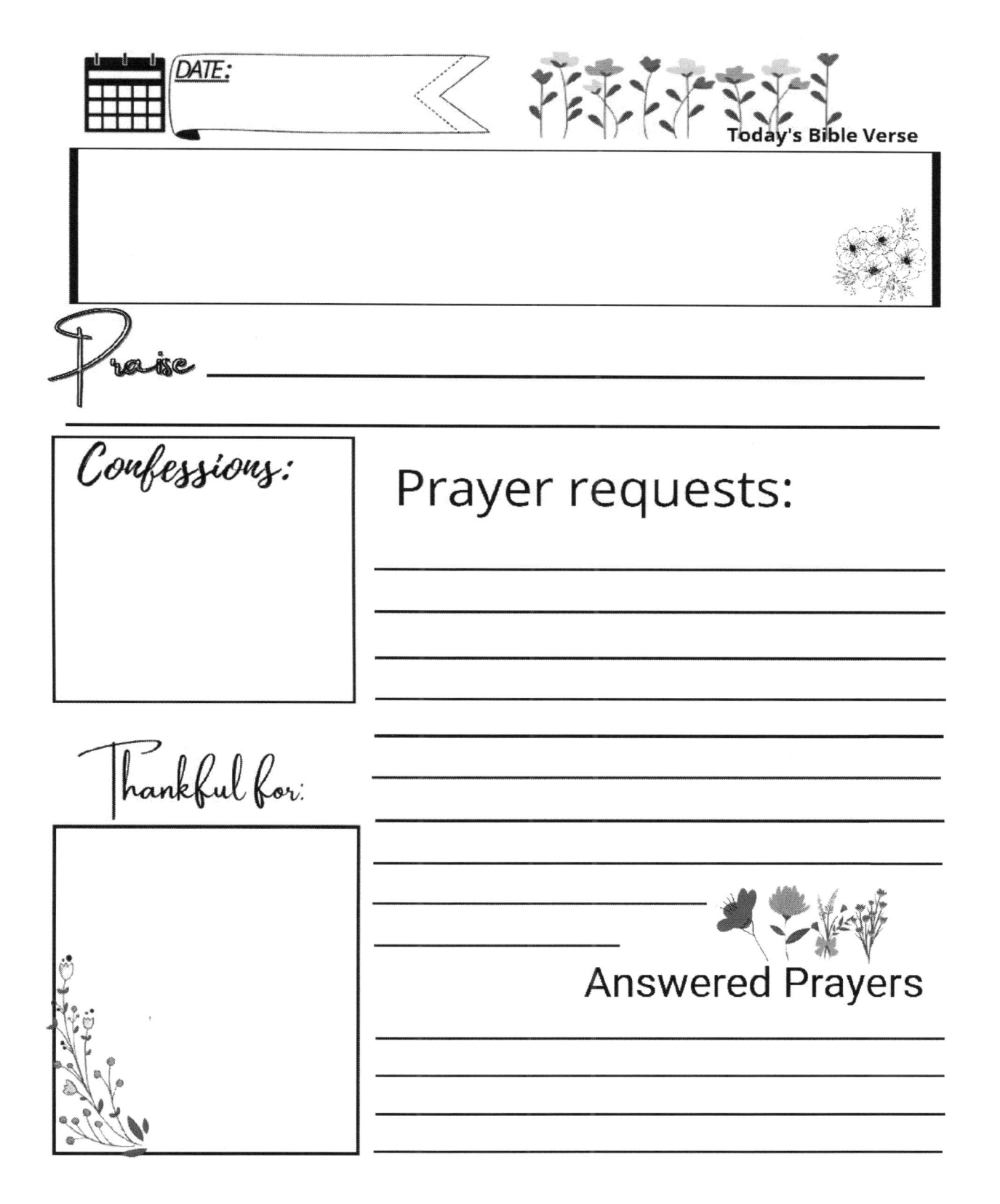

Today's Bible Verse

Praise _____

Confessions:

Prayer requests:

Thankful for:

Answered Prayers

DATE:

Today's Bible Verse

Praise _____

Confessions:

Prayer requests:
_____
_____
_____
_____
_____
_____
_____

Thankful for:

_____
_____

Answered Prayers
_____
_____
_____

DATE:

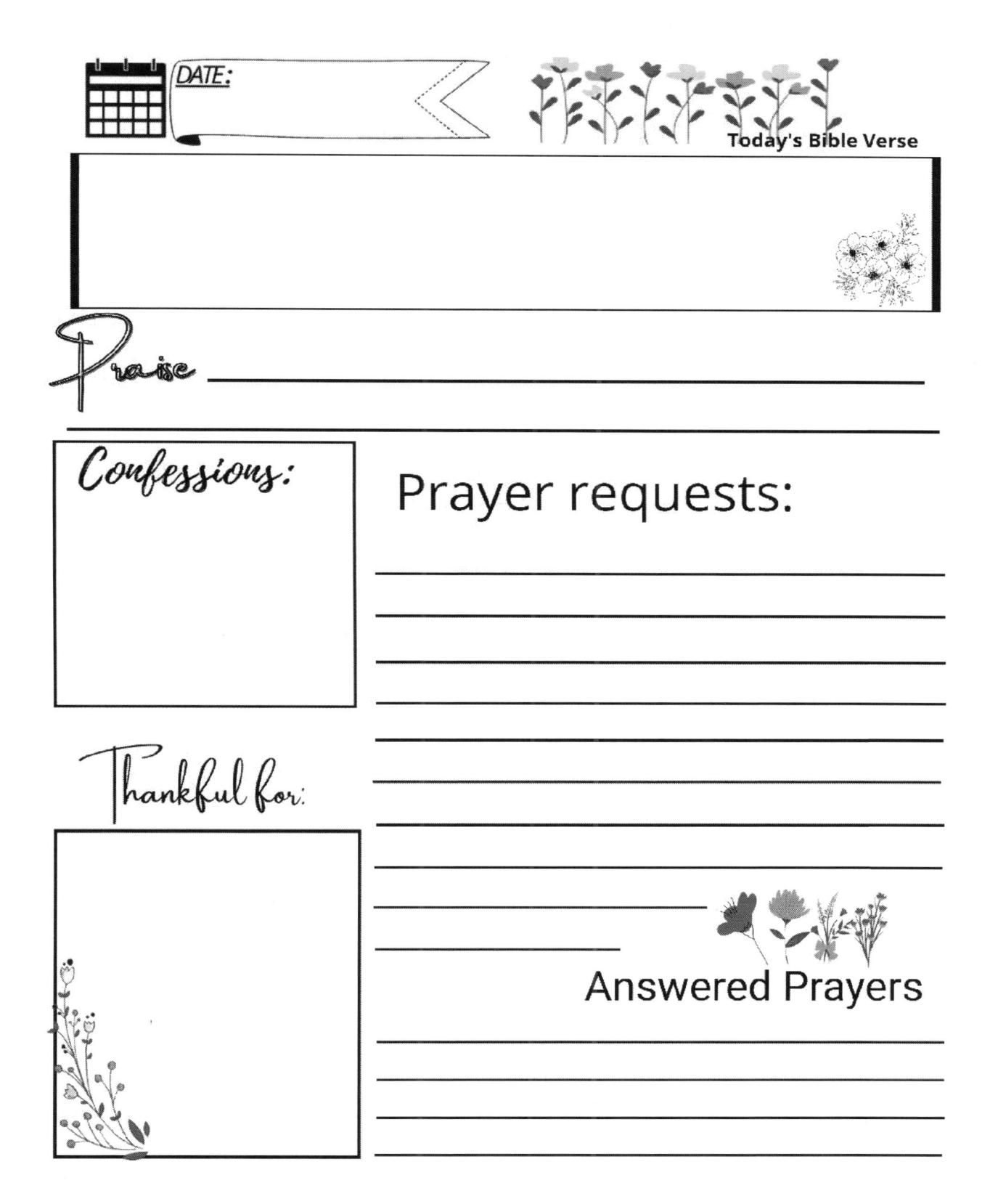

Today's Bible Verse

Praise _____

Confessions:

Prayer requests:

Thankful for:

Answered Prayers

DATE:

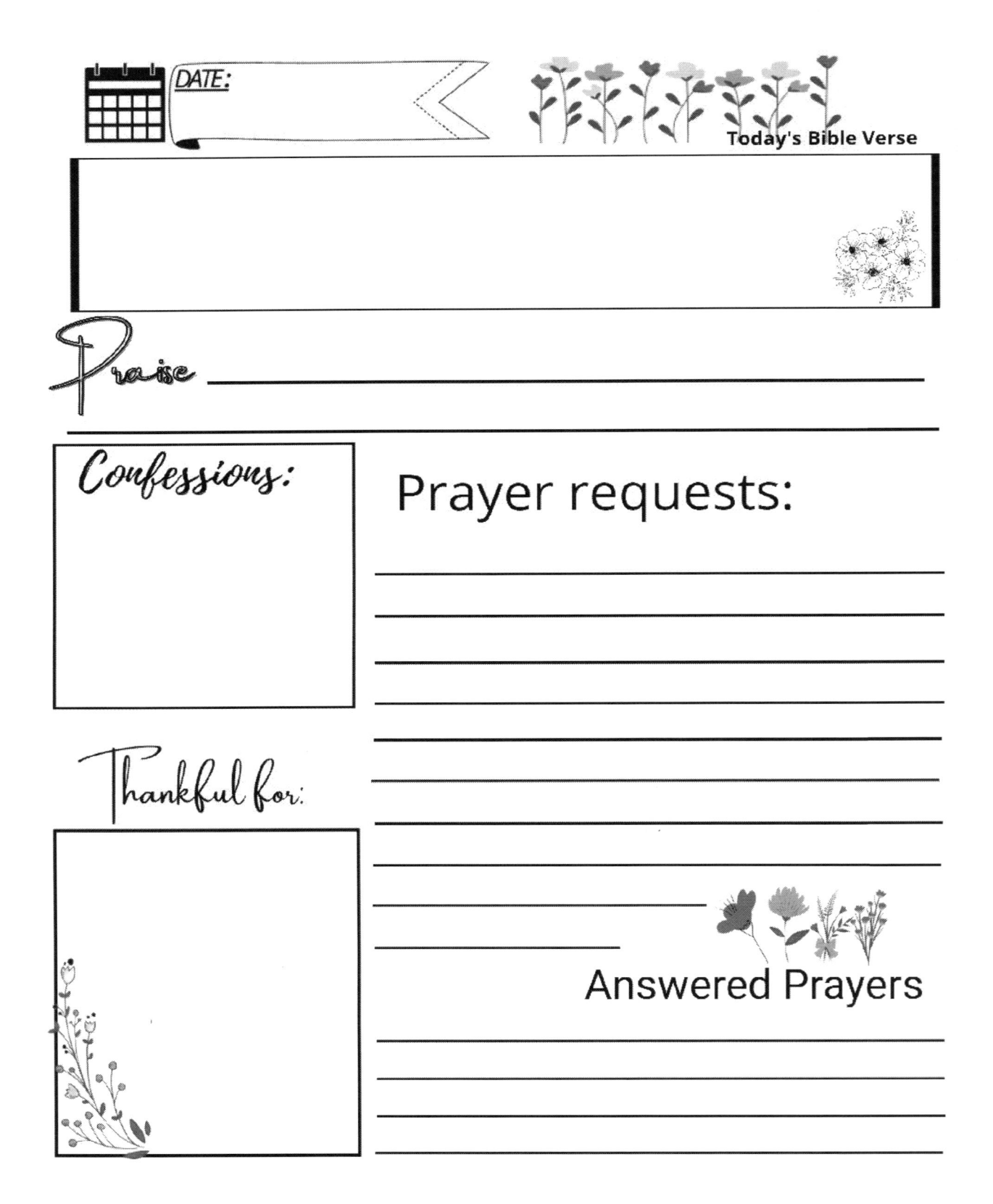

Today's Bible Verse

Praise _____

Confessions:

Prayer requests:

Thankful for:

Answered Prayers

DATE:

Today's Bible Verse

Praise _____

Confessions:

Prayer requests:

Thankful for:

Answered Prayers

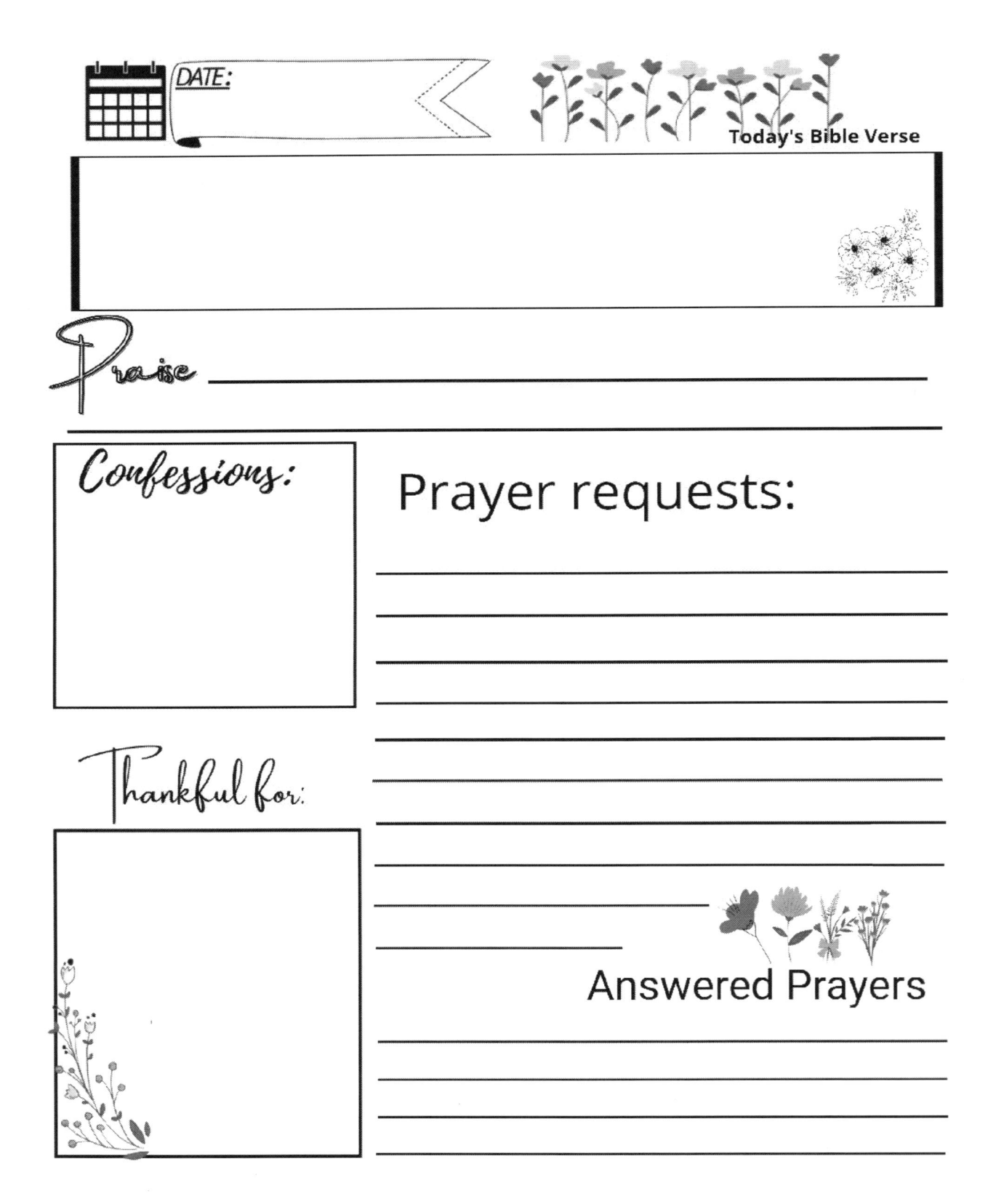

DATE:

Today's Bible Verse

Praise _____

Confessions:

Prayer requests:

Thankful for:

Answered Prayers

DATE:

Today's Bible Verse

Praise _____

Confessions:

Prayer requests:

Thankful for:

Answered Prayers

The Lord's Prayer

Jesus said;

In Matthew 6: 9-11 **9** *After this manner therefore pray ye:*

Our Father which art in heaven,

Hallowed be thy name.

Thy kingdom come, Thy will be done in earth, as it is in heaven.

Give us this day our daily bread.

And forgive us our debts, as we forgive our debtors. And lead us not into temptation, but deliver us from evil:

For thine is the kingdom, and the power, and the glory, for ever. Amen.

Testimonies

TESTIMONIES

Testimonies cont.

Well done for completing this Prayer Journal!

If you would like another one,

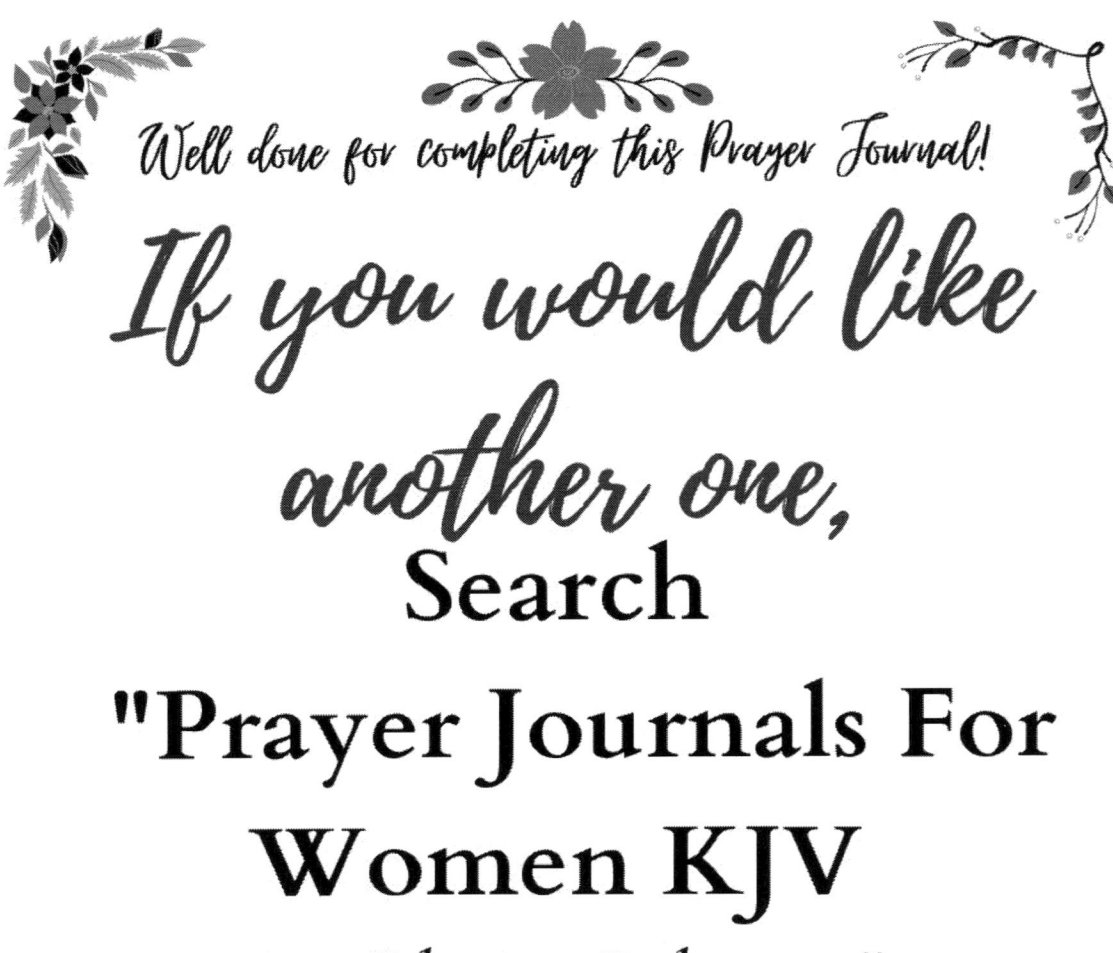

Search

"Prayer Journals For Women KJV

By Gloria Coleman"

on Amazon Where you are!

& If you would like to help us out,
Please leave us a review!
Thank you!

Made in the USA
Las Vegas, NV
01 December 2022